THE
LOYALISTS

BY THE SAME AUTHOR

HISTORY

GOODBYE TO GUNPOWDER
THE BIRTH OF THE CONSTITUTION
JULY 4, 1776
VALLEY FORGE
THE BATTLE OF NEW ORLEANS
VICTORY AT YORKTOWN
THE GREAT SEPARATION
THE TIDE TURNS
THE SIEGE OF BOSTON
THE WAR IN THE NORTH
THE GREAT CONSPIRACY
THE WAR WITH MEXICO
THE CALIFORNIA GOLD RUSH
THE FRENCH AND INDIAN WAR
THE WAR IN THE SOUTH
LEWIS AND CLARK
THE PANAMA CANAL
THE SPANISH-AMERICAN WAR
THE WARS IN BARBARY
LOUISIANA PURCHASE

BIOGRAPHY

ELIZABETH I
A Great Life in Brief

JOHN THE GREAT
The Times and Life of John L. Sullivan

THE GENTLEMAN FROM NEW YORK
A Biography of Roscoe Conkling

SIR HUMPHREY GILBERT
Elizabeth's Racketeer

SIR WALTER RALEIGH
That Damned Upstart

MARLBOROUGH
The Portrait of a Conqueror

BONNIE PRINCE CHARLIE
A Biography of the Young Pretender

THE
LOYALISTS

The Story of Those Americans Who
Fought Against Independence

by Donald Barr Chidsey

Illustrated

CROWN PUBLISHERS, INC., NEW YORK

© 1973 BY DONALD BARR CHIDSEY

LIBRARY OF CONGRESS CATALOG CARD NUMBER: 73-79619

ISBN: 0-517-504200

PRINTED IN THE UNITED STATES OF AMERICA

PUBLISHED SIMULTANEOUSLY IN CANADA BY
GENERAL PUBLISHING COMPANY LIMITED

*All illustrations courtesy
New York Public Library Picture Collection*

"The point at issue was a very subtle and refined one, and it required a great deal of mismanagement to make the quarrel irreconcilable."

Lord Acton, *Lectures on Modern History*

Contents

CHRONOLOGY ix
1 HATE THY BROTHER 1
2 TWO IMPROBABLE POLITICIANS 8
3 STICKS AND STONES MAY BREAK MY BONES 27
4 THE CURIOUS CASE OF BENJAMIN CHURCH 41
5 NO SPLASH IN THE SEWER 51
6 THE WAR MOVES SOUTH 62
7 BIG MAN IN BAVARIA 71
8 AN ABOMINATION BEFORE THE LORD 81
9 ALL THE GOOD AMERICANS 93
10 SO GROTESQUE A BLUNDER 106
11 THE INCONVENIENT ABORIGINES 114
12 "THE HEART WHICH IS CONSCIOUS OF ITS OWN
   RECTITUDE" 128
13 NIGHTMARE IN NEWBURGH 142
14 "TO LIE FOR HIS COUNTRY" 155
15 A TRAGEDY OF ERRORS 165
16 YOU CAN'T GO HOME AGAIN 172
NOTES 182
BIBLIOGRAPHY 193
INDEX 210

Contents

Chronology

1698   William Penn advanced the first Plan of Union
1754   Albany Plan of Union
1763   Treaty ending Seven Years War (French and Indian War) gives all Canada to Great Britain
1765   August 26–27, Thomas Hutchinson's home wrecked
1768   April 3, first redcoats land in Boston
1769   Hutchinson became acting governor
1770   March 5, Boston Massacre
1771   March, Hutchinson became governor
1773   December 16, Boston Tea Party
1774   May, Intolerable Acts, also Quebec Act. Hutchinson went to England after Gage was appointed military governor

1775

April 19, Lexington-Concord; siege of Boston began
June 17, Bunker Hill
July 3, Washington takes command of Continental Army
November, Sons of Liberty raid on Rivington's Wall Street plant

1776

January 9, *Common Sense* published
March 17, British evacuate Boston
July 4, Declaration of Independence
August 27, Battle of Long Island
November, Howe's bid to Patriots to become Loyalists

1777

September 26, British occupy Philadelphia
October 7, Burgoyne surrenders at Saratoga
December 25–26, Washington crosses Delaware, Battle of Trenton

1778

April-May, Carlyle peace commission
June 18, British evacuate Philadelphia

1780   October 7, Battle of King's Mountain
1781   October 18, Cornwallis surrenders at Yorktown
1782   November 30, signing of Peace of Paris

1

Hate Thy Brother

IT HAS BEEN SAID that nothing succeeds like success; and it could be added that few things fail like failure. The man who has lost a contest will never on that account become an object of awe, much less adoration, as so often does the winner, the hero.

The American Revolution was a civil war. British troops, the officers mostly English, the men Irish and Scottish, took some part in it; and so did the French, and uniformed louts from no fewer than six German principalities; but it was essentially a brother-against-brother affair, splitting families, turning cousins upon cousins, nephews against uncles, so that friends of many years' standing suddenly refused to speak to one another. (Jonathan Sewall, one of the many Loyalists who fled to Canada, was to change the spelling of his name to Sewell because, he said, he wished to distinguish himself from the members of the Whig branch of the family, whom he abhorred.)

Civil wars, traditionally, are the bitterest kind. There was little that was orthodox about this one, at least on the part of the Americans, to whom it was largely personal and entirely disagreeable. The hatreds that it engendered were to last a lifetime; enmity was to pursue the defeated clear to the grave, and even beyond. There was, after the Revolution, no forgiving slap of the loser's back on the part of the winner, with a "Better luck next time, old man!" Sportsmanship did not prevail. The animosity persisted. The ill will fed upon itself, refusing to fade.

Timothy Ruggles was a rugged Tory from the Massachusetts hinterland, a veteran of the Seven Years War, a brigadier in the miltia, an unpleasant man so outspoken in his political opinions that the neighbors took to poisoning his cattle. He attended the Stamp Act Congress of 1765, and indeed presided over it, but he refused to endorse its too-liberal resolutions. When Boston was besieged, after the day of Lexington and Concord, he went into the city and tried to raise an anti-colonial regiment, which he proposed to lead against the rebels. Yet his two brothers and several of his children were strong in the Whig cause.

Daniel Dulany, a distinguished attorney, thought that his fellow Marylanders were going too far when they approved of the Declaration of Independence, and he lined up on the opposite side. Most of his family went with him, but one son, Benjamin, was a Patriot.

All *three* of the sons of Lieutenant Governor William Bull of South Carolina were self-declared Patriots, though that official himself was a pronounced Tory.

Benjamin Franklin was a Patriot, but his son William was a prominent Loyalist, while *his* son, William Temple Franklin, was to serve as secretary to the Patriots' peace commission at Paris in 1782.

Thomas Heyward, a signer of the Declaration of Independence, was the son of a Tory.

The fat bookseller Henry Knox fell in love with Lucy Flucker, daughter of a Tory official who was described as "the most hated man in Boston," at the time of the siege. Secretly married, they slipped through the British lines, so that he could join the newly authorized Continental Army, in which he was to serve as chief of artillery.[1] She never saw her family again.

We do not know where these curious appellations came from. There were no organized, accepted political parties in colonial America, only temporary cliques and claques in the various legislatures, and these came and went.

Both "Tory" and "Whig" were originally pejorative and borrowed without acknowledgment from the English, though they were not born there. "Whig" meant, originally, a country bumpkin, a hayseed, and soon afterward a Scottish raider, or irregular thief, a Whiggamore. "Tory" was an anglicization of the Gaelic *toraidhe,* meaning literally "pursued man," more often bogtrotter, rapparee, outlaw. It was an Irish word—and low Irish at that.

In America, when Americans began to feel the necessity of asserting themselves in a political manner, these words— nobody knows how—came to mean, more or less, liberal and conservative. The Whigs were liberals, the Tories the others. The Whigs in America preferred to call themselves Patriots, the Tories preferred to call themselves Loyalists; and by these names they shall be known in this book, but it must not be supposed that there is any sense in them.

"A brother offended is harder to be won than a strong city" goes a saying. At this distance it is not possible to see why the Loyalists of the Revolution should be viewed with such rancor by those who were not Loyalists; but there is no doubt that they were.

What kind of people were they? This is a matter that was in dispute at the time and has been in dispute ever since.

The immediate thought is that the Loyalists would be the large landowners, the propertied. But this was only partly true—true, as it were, in spots. Most of those who chose the King's side, at a sacrifice, were indeed men of conservative views, though they did not necessarily number among themselves the land's richest, as popular opinion had it, nor did they include the most eminent among the learned and the professionals. Tears have been shed over the belief that America by kicking over the royal traces lost forever some of her finest minds and most admirable managers, and a parallel is drawn with the exodus of all those talented Huguenots who were forced out of France by the revocation of the Edict of Nantes. This parallel is not exact.

There are no figures, but it would be safe to say that four of the richest men in America at the time of the outbreak of the Revolution were George Washington, Charles Carroll of Carrollton, Philip Schuyler, and John Hancock. All four of these were pronounced Patriots, and never wavered in that belief. Two signed the Declaration of Independence; the other two were generals in the Continental Army.

The colonies best known for widespread acres, for landlords of almost unlimited holdings, were Virginia and New York. The rule that big owners favored the King—if there ever was such a rule—falls apart here. New York probably contained a larger percentage of Loyalists than any other colony, but Virginia certainly contained the smallest such percentage, and was, in fact, almost unanimously anti-throne.

The newly-arrives were, as a rule, Loyalists. Very often they were officeholders, appointed by and removable by the Crown, and it was no more than natural that they should take that side. A total of 2,560 Loyalists were to petition the special Parliamentary commission for compensation of their losses in the war, and of these almost two thirds were not native Americans.

The same thing applied to Anglican ministers in the

American colonies, who were accustomed to praying for the royal family every Sunday, at least, and conceived themselves to be under vow to the House of Hanover. Most of the non-Anglican ministers were Whiggish. There were exceptions, both ways. Virginia and Maryland were the only American colonies in which the Church of England was an established institution, an inherent part of the state, yet of the hundred Episcopal ministers in Virginia at the outbreak of the war eleven became members of local committees of safety while one became a brigadier general (and not a chaplain, either) in the Continental Army.

The Loyalists were widespread. They called no one section their own, but were represented, if sometimes feebly in every colony, in every state. More than a third of those who sought compensation after the war were from New York. South Carolina was the second for its proportion of Loyalists to total population, and the others were evenly distributed, down to New Hampshire, the last.

The Germans have a saying: *Wes Brot ich ess, des Lied ich sing:* Whose bread I eat his song I sing. This was not the case with the Germans who had recently been pouring into the American colonies, most of them into Pennsylvania. Unlike so many of the other come-latelys they did not favor the royal cause; yet neither did they cheer for the Whigs; they remained sturdily non-partisan, a hard thing to do in those days, and it was an attitude that caused both sides to be suspicious of them. Many were opposed to war—the Mennonites, Pietists, Dunkards, Moravians, Schwenkfelders—and in this they found themselves in sympathy with their neighbors, the well-entrenched Quakers, who also did not believe in fighting or in taking oaths. Like the Quakers they were excused from doing military duty, though most of them were obliged to pay special taxes to offset this.

How many Tories were there in America? We will

never know. Lecky [2] has affirmed that the American Revolution was "the work of an energetic minority, who succeeded in committing an undecided and fluctuating majority to courses for which they had little love, and leading them step by step to a position from which it was impossible to recede," but of course Lecky was never there himself.

John Adams is the man most often quoted in this connection. He gave it as his opinion that at the outset of the war the colonials were almost evenly divided one third Patriots, one third Loyalist, while the last third was made up of men who didn't give a damn one way or the other. This statement is suspiciously pat. Adams made it in a letter to a friend, many years after the war was over. He did not pretend that it was an exact estimate, but offered it only as an impression; and he was a very emotional man.

A more recent authority avers: "The problem of discovering how many Tories there were is complicated, moreover, by there having been, between avowed supporters and avowed opponents of the Revolution, a great middle group of passive citizens who had no clear point of view, who hoped perhaps that one side or the other would win, but who wanted above all not to be disturbed." [3]

This can be doubted. Halfway measures were against the rules of the Revolutionary game. Even the Loyalists, and most emphatically the Whigs, refused to recognize neutrality, their belief being that "those that ain't for us are agin us," with no middle ground.

Even if Adams's division is accepted, it is subject to shadings: "The total number of Loyalists in the population has traditionally been put at one third, following John Adams, but if *active* Loyalists are meant, this proportion is a maximum, probably too high: the true figure would seem to lie somewhere between a minimum of 13 and a maximum of 30 per cent of the whole population, or between 15 and 36 per cent of the *white* population. (These figures include men, women, and children.)" [4]

Figures don't lie, it has been said, but liars figure. In June of 1778 Delaware listed forty-six especially objectionable Tories, men who were to be excepted from any possible future pardon, and these included three physicians, one lawyer, seven officeholders, nine husbandmen, one bricklayer, one saddler, three shallopmen, one hatter, two innkeepers, a fairly good cross-section of any colony's population, and most certainly no elite.

The soundest tables we possess are those compiled in three years of work by the Parliamentary commission on compensation, which show that of the claimants 49.1 percent were farmers, 9.8 percent artisans, 18.6 percent merchants and shopkeepers, 10.1 percent officeholders, only 9.1 percent professional men.

The cream of the colonial population had not been scraped off.

2

Two Improbable Politicians

THOMAS HUTCHINSON was one of those men who, if history had only let them alone, would have shone bright in the eyes of posterity.

When he moved, which he did ponderously, Hutchinson's titles must have clacked against one another like chain mail, like so many steel plates. He was at various times lieutenant governor of Massachusetts, judge of the probate court of Suffolk County, chief justice of the provincial supreme court, captain of Castle William in Boston Harbor, president of the Massachusetts council of state, and sundry other things too numerous to mention, a veritable Pooh-Bah. The as-yet-unwritten lines about his hometown

> Here's to the city of Boston!
> The home of the bean and the cod.
> Where the Cabots speak only to Lowells
> And the Lowells speak only to God.

would not have amused him. He would have lifted well-plucked eyebrows, to ask: "Who *are* the Cabots?" And a moment later: "And who are the Lowells?" In his day it was the Lyndes, the Olivers, the Vassalls, and the Hutchinsons, especially the Hutchinsons.

Here was no stuffed shirt! The lieutenant governor did not owe his position to a supple spine and calloused knees brought about by groveling before Majesty. He was no hanger-on at court. He had been born right there in the Massachusetts Bay colony, of a family long established in those parts and always eminent. He was a great-grandson of Anne Hutchinson, the famous antinomian exile, regarded by many still, in the late eighteenth century, as a saint. He had inherited money, and he had made more. He was a successful merchant in a land that admired its merchants. His estate at nearby Milton was a showplace, a model, both garden and farm. He was a reserved man, not well liked, never cheered in the streets, and sometimes described as a fish; but he was a wizard with figures and more than once had saved vast sums of money for the province he served— he and his cousins and in-laws—so long and so faithfully.

Connecticut and Rhode Island were privileged colonies, the only ones allowed to elect their own governors. The governor of Massachusetts, like the lieutenant governor, was appointed by the King and removable by him at will, though the colony paid his salary. The governor in the 1760s was Francis Bernard, an Oxford man, who told a good story and was a gifted amateur architect. His wife was a cousin of Lord Barrington, who was usually secretary of war. They had eight children. Bernard was not a crook, nor was he a fool, but he was more interested in his own financial affairs than in the well-being of his constituents, being in this in the conventional gubernatorial pattern. His chief concern was to keep out of trouble. The job paid £1,100 a year. Bernard had enough put away so that he was ready to retire, if he could do so with grace. For a long while he had been angling for a title. The political situation in all of the American colonies, but particularly in Massachusetts, had been smoldering ever since the end of the French and Indian War, with the home country making plans to tax them. Bernard wanted to get out of Massachusetts before the lid blew off.

It was taken for granted that when he went he would be succeeded as governor by the present Number Two man of Massachusetts, Thomas Hutchinson.

The Number *Three* man was the colonial secretary, Andrew Oliver, who happened to be a brother-in-law of Hutchinson.

This was the official hierarchy. *U*nofficially the Number One man was the clerk of the lower house of the General Court, which is what the legislature was called in Massachusetts. The person in that position ordinarily did not wield much power; but this one did, and indeed he was systematically preparing to overthrow the governor, to bring about the explosion that Francis Bernard feared.

He was an extraordinarily ordinary man, a rickle of sticks unskillfully assembled. He was pale, thin, and had a sallow complexion, wishy-washy gray eyes, a throat all cords, and clothes that were drab. His lips twitched, and his hands were never still, palsy's fault. His name was Samuel Adams. A more unlikely Founding Father it would be hard to imagine.

Thomas Hutchinson called him the Machiavel of Chaos. Yet his manner was quiet, kindly, low-keyed; and though he mixed with the riffraff he never forgot that he was a Harvard man. He was deeply religious, an old-fashioned Puritan.

History has labeled Samuel Adams the Great Rabble-rouser, the Great Spellbinder, but a man with a high reedy voice like his—a voice that quavered when he raised it—could not truly have been that. This fellow frequented the coffeehouses as well as street corners, but though he was at all times counting votes he never did this aloud. He was the originator of American machine politics. Smeared as a radical, in fact he was an arch-conservative. He never stood on a soapbox or a stump. He would speak from the floor of a legislative chamber whenever he thought that a speech was called for; but he abjured magniloquent periods, and when he was finished he sat down.[5]

Samuel Adams virtually invented independence in America. Before his time it had been a dirty word.

Today we would call him a rigger, a schemer. His associates praised him as a master worker "out-of-doors." It was a phrase of the time, and not opprobrious. To work out-of-doors meant to get legislative things lined up before the opposition had done so, to have one's course charted before the opening gavel banged against its block. It meant buttonholing, whispering promises, perhaps half breathing threats. Had legislative halls then included lobbies, Samuel Adams would have been hailed as the first great lobbyist. But he could work *in*doors as well, and did. He served on all sorts of committees. He took no vacation, knew no holiday. He was always there.

He was not serpentine, but a straightforward thinker. His words, whether written or spoken—and he was a prodigious writer—never wobbled; there was no touch of the weasel in them. He saw his fight, and he faced it. The royal charter that had been granted to the colonists of Massachusetts Bay was being violated by the English ministers of the Crown, and the violation must be resisted. It was as simple as that. The rights of his fellow countrymen, their inalienable rights as Englishmen, were about to be taken from them, chipped away. This must not be permitted. He, Samuel Adams, was not a radical, Heaven forbid. The Tories were the radicals, the men in Whitehall.

A failure in business, penniless, he flaunted his poverty as if it were some sort of proud polychromatic oriflamme, symbolic of his cause. Sartorially he was a disgrace. Penury,

Samuel Adams

however, never fazed him. Of the various municipal and provincial jobs he held, only one, the clerkship of the Massachusetts House of Representatives, paid a salary; and this varied, though it averaged somewhat less than £100 a year.

It did not need to be so. He could have sold out. The King's party undoubtedly approached Samuel Adams with offers, though there is no record of this: such things are not recorded unless and until they are consummated. Perhaps Adams did not even know what was happening? He might have become rich. Despite his blatantly unpeerlike appearance he might have become a baronet, or at least a knight. It never occurred to him.

Washington has been called the Father of his Country, and this is surely fair. But it would not be irreverent, nor yet inaccurate, to call Samuel Adams the country's grandfather. Without the groundwork he laid, you and I would never have heard of George Washington.

Samuel Adams shared with his second cousin John, the up-and-coming young Braintree lawyer who was thinking of moving to Boston, where the action was, a great-grandfather, Henry Adams, a Devonshire farmer who had come to the New World in 1636. His own father, Deacon Samuel, Sr., had been a busy officeholder—tithingman, assessor, selectman, constable, and a member of the legislature, also, briefly, hogreeve, though there were very few hogs left in Boston at the time. Deacon Samuel was one of the organizers of the Caucus Club.[6] It was with men like this—caulkers, ropemakers, joiners, sailmakers—that the son mostly mixed. This infuriated Thomas Hutchinson, who thought that it was a sin for a man born to a better position to descend to be what he, the lieutenant governor, called the commonality. Hutchinson did not have delusions of grandeur: that's the way he had been brought up; and he looked upon the clerk of the lower house as a traitor to his class, which is to say the worst traitor of all.

Even Thomas Hutchinson had to admit that the Caucus clubs (there were three of them by this time: the North End, the middle, and the South End) were a force to be considered. In fact they controlled Boston politically; and Samuel Adams controlled the Caucus clubs.

As clerk of the lower house it was Adams's custom to write all its official papers in his own hand, which hand it would seem never grew weary, for he was writing regularly for a large field of periodicals under more than twenty pen-names; and he saw to it that no chance to assert his belief in the colonial rights was lost, howsoever seemingly slight it might be. Thus, he always referred to the hall in which the legislature met not as the Town House, its proper name, but as the State House. He would refer to the "laws of the land" rather than to the provincial laws. He would write of the debates as "Parliamentary" debates, as distinct, it would seem, from those that took place in the *British* Parliament, as Adams invariably called it. These things made the lieutenant governor squirm, but that was all that he *could* do. Most provocative of all were the secretary's references to the colonial charter as "the compact," implying that it was no privilege granted by the King but rather an agreement openly arrived at between equals.

These were pinpricks, they were fleabites. Yet they were applied with all the earnestness of the zealot and never in a clownish spirit of fun; for Samuel Adams, like Thomas Hutchinson, had no sense of humor. They fought grimly, these two, and most of the time in silence, though the lieutenant governor sometimes could be heard gnashing his teeth. The lieutenant governor had a handsome professional smile that he was always prepared to turn on for the benefit of anybody whose social status warranted this favor; and

The Stamp Act provoked mob action throughout the colonies.

Adams had a rather pleasant singing voice, a high tenor, which he liked to raise at family get-togethers and at pot-waving jollifications in the back rooms of waterfront taverns; but neither man had ever learned to laugh.

The Stamp Act of 1765 seemed harmless enough when it was enacted. It had not been a hasty thing. It had been framed to raise some revenue from the American colonies without hurting their economy, and it had been read to the various colonial agents in London, who were allowed time to consult at long distance with their governments, asking for instructions. Nobody seemed to have had much against the act. Yet when it was passed, when it became a law, it raised a yell of rage in America.

The colonists vowed to abstain from the use of stamps, and, more immediately, they called upon the men appointed to distribute these stamps to resign under threat of tar-and-feathers, so that when the stamps did arrive in the colonies there was nobody to receive them. There was a great deal of trouble attendant upon these resignations, and all up and down the coast the colonists suddenly appeared to be almost on the edge of open revolt. The government, amazed and hurt, backed down. The Stamp Act was repealed. The colonists cheered.

Both Governor Bernard and Lieutenant Governor Hutchinson had opposed the passage of the Stamp Act, which they thought ill-advised, but their opposition, from that great distance, had gone to waste. They did not publicize it. Once the act had been passed they thought it their duty to enforce it, no matter what might be their personal opinions, and they said this. Thomas Hutchinson especially said it, again and again; for he was no man to be silent about anything to do with his duty. He stood on his dignity. He refused to admit in public that he had opposed the passage of a Parliamentary act, and when the word spread through Massachusetts that he and the governor actually had *urged* the Stamp Act upon Parliament neither man would lower himself with a denial. The result was that the rumor, prodded by the indefatigable Samuel Adams by means of his many newspaper outlets,[7] and perhaps even started by him in the first place, grew to such a size that it was no longer recognizable as a rumor but appealed to most citizens as a naked fact. Indeed, in the popular belief Hutchinson—though not Bernard—had even helped to *frame* the hated piece of legislation. He would not deny this. He wouldn't discuss it at all.

The matter was given a personal turn, making it that much worse in Massachusetts, when it was announced that the stamp distributor for that colony would be Andrew Oliver, the colonial treasurer, Thomas Hutchinson's brother-

British stamp issued under the Stamp Act

in-law. A group of North Enders under the leadership of
Ebenezer Mackintosh, a lantern-jawed, long-legged cobbler,
hanged Oliver in effigy from the Liberty Tree, a huge elm
in Hanover Square, Boston. Governor Bernard ordered Sheriff Greenleaf to cut it down, but Greenleaf, after one look
at the lay-out, reported back that such an act would be as
much as his life was worth. So the dummy dangled there
all day, and after sunset the North Enders themselves cut
it down and took it to Andrew Oliver's dock at the foot of
Kilby Street, where the treasurer had started to put up a
wooden building. Oliver had intended this to be a block of
shops, as a speculation, but the members of the mob supposed that it was planned as a stamp office, a place of distribution. They took it apart. They carried the planks and
beams and shingles up to the top of Beacon Hill, where they
made a bonfire of them. There too they beheaded the effigy
of Oliver and cast this upon the flames. Still they weren't
satisfied, so they started for Oliver's house.

Thomas Hutchinson and Sheriff Greenleaf tried to intercept them, to talk some sense into them, but a shower of
stones cut *that* short. Oliver had been warned, and his house
was empty. The gangsters went through it like locusts.
They smashed the windows and the furniture; they smashed
what was said to be the largest looking-glass in North America; they drank or stole all of the liquor and wine; and then
they vanished.

The next day Andrew Oliver publicly promised to resign as soon as his appointment came, and when it *did* come
he did the same thing all over again, by the side of the Liberty Tree, before a jeering crowd.

It was Thomas Hutchinson's turn next. Less than two
weeks after the attack upon the treasurer's home the mobs
were out again, two of them this time, though Mackintosh
was in general charge. They wrecked the elegant new house
of Benjamin Hallowell, the comptroller of customs, and stole

Thomas Hutchinson

all of his wine. They started to do the same thing at the home of Charles Paxton, marshal of the court of vice-admiralty, but he talked them into retiring to a nearby bar, where he bought drinks all around, and they left him alone after that. This second mob, led by Mackintosh in person, tore through the home of William Story, the register of the vice-admiralty court, and wrecked it, after first making a fire of all the court papers they could find.

Then the two mobs got together and started up toward Thomas Hutchinson's large square white house in Garden Court Street.

It was still early in the evening, and the family was at dinner. They heard the mob coming. The lieutenant governor chased them all, together with the servants, out of a back door, whispering to them where they should go. He had barricaded the front door, and he meant to stand behind it. He was sixty-two years old.

Probably he would have been killed, for the mob was not in a playful mood. His elder daughter saved him. She refused to go to the assigned hiding-place but returned to the house and tugged at her father's arm, vowing that if he wouldn't come away she would stay there with him. That did it. They both ran.

Seconds later the North Enders broke in. They had axes now, and they went mad. The story among them was that the Stamp Act had been *conceived and framed* right here in this very house, and they set about their work in a frenzy. They broke all of the windows, upstairs and down, smashed all of the furniture, slashed the wall hangings to ribbons, slashed the paintings. They stole about £900 in cash from a strongbox, and they also stole the silver and of course the wine. They went out into the garden, chopped down all the trees, and uprooted the bushes. From the lieutenant governor's study they took all the papers they could carry, including the first draft of the second volume of his irreplaceable *History of the Province of Massachusetts-Bay*, a job on which he had spent thirty years; and these they carried outside, presumably meaning to burn them, but a rainstorm caused them to give up this plan, so they scattered the papers broadcast.[8]

The rain did not keep them from trying to pull the building apart. Nothing less, it would seem, would satisfy them. They tried to batter down the partitions between the rooms. They climbed to the roof and tried to tear off the huge cupola that surmounted the house, and when they could not budge this they started to rip off the roof itself: it was made of slate.

The rain had ceased, and when daylight found them thus engaged they scattered, scurrying away. Creatures like this do not like the light.

Mackintosh was picked up the next day, questioned briefly, and let go. A few others were questioned, but nobody was formally arrested, and no charges were made.

Hutchinson put in a bill for indemnity, asking £3,194 17s 6d, for he had figured the thing down to the last dessert spoon. The General Court ordered the prompt payment of this bill, thanks to Samuel Adams, but there was a rider in the grant: nobody was to be prosecuted for the attack. Governor Bernard signed it reluctantly, knowing that if he did not his friend would get nothing at all. King George, months later, disallowed this grant [9] with its shameful condition; but this did no good, for by that time the money had been paid.

(It must not be supposed that Samuel Adams had anything to do with the wrecking of the Hutchinson house. There was nothing crude about the man, who indeed was famous for his finesse; and when he did venture into violence it was with a move so carefully planned and so skillfully executed that it has served as a shining example to all future revolutionaries—the Boston Tea Party.)

Bernard was at last recalled to England, ostensibly "for consultation," actually, as everybody knew, to be made a baronet; and this left Thomas Hutchinson, in 1769, as acting governor. He did not become full, in-fact governor until March of 1771, at which time Andrew Oliver of course was moved into the lieutenant governorship.

Samuel Adams is known best in history as the man who devised the smooth-functioning system of committees of correspondence, which made the Revolution possible. He was better known by his own generation as the Man of the Town Meeting.

Tacitus tells us that the ancient Germans used to debate every important question twice in council—once when they were drunk and again when they were sober. One time was enough for the old New Englanders, as it is for their descendants today.

Historians avow that the town meeting, which has been hailed as democracy in its purest form, is directly derived from the old English folkmote or -moot, from which, etymologists add, we get our expression "moot point," meaning a doubtful point, one that should be taken up at the next moot.[10] This institution must have existed in Druidical England when the Angles and the Saxons, the Frisians and Jutes, still roamed that thick-forested land; but it died without a trace under the heel of the haughty Norman, only to be resurrected hundreds of years later, nobody knows how, in America in the form of the New England town meeting.

The adult male residents of a given community, provided that they owned some manner of property, would gather together regularly at least once a year, and talk, and argue, fixing their own tax rate, arranging their own affairs. Since it was the way they wished to conduct themselves, and since they had no manner of aristocracy or elected or hereditary rulers, this right was written into the royal charter granted to the province of Massachusetts Bay. The early colonial Patriots were purists; they believed in the letter of the law, taking the charter *in toto*, literally. Largely as a result of the Puritan revolution in England and later the so-called Glorious Revolution of 1688, the real power there had shifted from the Crown to Parliament; but the colonists had nothing to do with this, and they insisted upon following their old ways.

The New England town meeting too had changed, but this was a *permissible* change, since it was not specifically forbidden—as indeed it had not been anticipated—by the charter. The town meeting in Boston soon did much more than administer the affairs of the town. It adopted resolutions on matters of international importance. It disapproved of Parliamentary actions, protesting them. It arrogated unto itself powers never meant for it; and all the smaller town meetings throughout Massachusetts, and soon everywhere else in New England, did the same. Egged on by Samuel Adams, Boston set the pace.

The town meeting was Adams's metier, his chief tool. He led it as a maestro might lead a symphony orchestra. He corresponded with the leaders of the smaller communities, advising them. He set in motion the machinery by means of which to call all sorts of special sessions, until at last the thing was practically a continuous body. He had no right to do this, but he did it, while Hutchinson fumed. Often Adams was himself the moderator of the meeting in Boston, or, if not, he was the secretary. In any event he and the fellow members of the various Caucus clubs, having consulted in advance, knew just what they wanted; and usually they got it.

The Boston town meeting was imperceptibly enlarged

to include the surrounding towns, another move for which there was no authority; but Governor Hutchinson protested in vain. The town meetings of Roxbury, Dorchester, Brookline, Cambridge, and Charlestown were invited to join up with that of Boston, and they accepted, forming a powerful if extra-legal body. Men no longer called it "town meeting," but knew it now as "the Body."

Massachusetts like all of the other colonies had property qualifications for voting, but these were liberal and were not strictly enforced. Boston had about fifteen hundred qualified voters, yet town meetings attended by three thousand and even four thousand were not unusual. Often the crowd was too big for Faneuil Hall and the meeting was moved to the nearby Old South Church, the largest building in town. Hutchinson complained to Lord Hillsborough, the bigot in London who was currently in charge of administering the affairs of America, that "there is scarce ever any inquiry, and anything with the appearance of a man is admitted without scrutiny." Even Loyalists would have been let in, though they would do well to keep their mouths shut.

Shaken in his carapace, but always too proud to let anxiety show, Thomas Hutchinson, who never had been popular, scarcely dared to venture out-of-doors. He had become the epitome of oppression; and when at last he was called to England "for consultation" there was no farewell party, no bands played, nor did cannon boom; so that he departed in an utter, sullen silence.

The military commander in America, Lieutenant General Thomas Gage, would become governor in Thomas Hutchinson's absence. For of course Hutchinson would be back. As every Loyalist knew, this blow-up soon would be over, this dust storm would subide, and the King would come into his own again.

Two British regiments debarking on Boston's Long Wharf in 1768 to restore order. Engraving by Paul Revere

In England, Hutchinson was offered a baronetcy, but he declined on the ground that he could not afford to support the dignity. The war, which was virtually in existence by this time, would ruin his trading business, and he feared that the rebels, in command all over the colony outside of Boston itself, would confiscate his lovely place in Milton, as indeed they did, branding him a traitor. He was given an honorary degree by Oxford. He was addressed as "governor" and "your excellency" everywhere, and people openly sympathized with him. He met the King several times. He called upon or was called upon by Lords North, Rockingham, Hillsborough, Mansfield, Hardwicke, Dartmouth, Wedderburn. His advice was solicited about the American colonies, and his opinions were listened to. He was a very unhappy man. He died 3 July 1780, a stranger in a strange land, unwept, unsung. He had done his duty as he saw it, but that was not enough. He had been born too late.

3

Sticks and Stones May Break My Bones

Parliament's most ferocious speechmaker, Isaac Barré, a man reputed to carry vinegar in his mouth instead of spit, once turned aside in the Commons to partake of a little refreshment. "My God," a backbencher was heard to murmur. "Does it eat biscuit? I thought it only ate raw meat."

Colonel Barré looked the part. He was swarthy, and he glared. A bullet had smashed his face, on the left side, breaking the cheekbone, closing the eye to a mere glittering slit, and it had left a scar that pulsed when the colonel was angry, which was most of the time. He was an Irishman of French extraction and had been a career officer until his wound, which was causing him to go blind, drove him out of active army service and into politics. He had been with Wolfe at Quebec; it was there that he was hit. He knew the Americans and liked them.

The Americans, in turn, liked him. Most of their so-called champions in Parliament were eccentric, to say the least of it, and despite a great deal of iridescent oratory they did little for America—the sonorous Burke, the accipitrine Pitt, and Wilkes the jumping jack—but you always knew where you stood with good old damn-your-eyes Isaac Barré.[11]

"Keep your hands out of the pockets of the Americans and they will be obedient subjects," he had told the Commons. His strictures, to be sure, had no more effect upon the solons than had the more mellifluous outpourings of Pitt and Burke, but Americans understood them better. It was Colonel Barré, too, who had given them that beloved phrase, Sons of Liberty.

The Honorable Charles ("Champagne Charlie") Townshend, at a debate on the proposed Stamp Act, in the Commons 7 February 1765, had provoked it. He had spoken in favor of the act, and finished:

"These children of our own planting, nourished by our indulgence until they are grown to a good degree of strength and opulence, and protected by our arms, will they grudge to contribute their mite to relieve us from the heavy load of national expense which we lie under?"

Barré was on his feet instantly.

Children planted by your care? No! Your opposition planted them in America; they fled from your tyranny into a then uncultivated land, where they were exposed to almost all the hardships to which human nature is liable, and, among others, to the savage cruelty of the enemy of the country—a people the most subtle, and, I take it upon me to say, the most truly terrible of any people that ever inhabited any part of God's earth; and yet, actuated by principles of true English liberty, they met all these hardships with pleasure, compared with those they suffered in their own country from the hands of those that should have been their friends.

They nourished up by your indulgence? They grew by your neglect of them. As soon as you began to care about them, that care was exercised in sending persons to rule over them, in one department and another, who were perhaps the deputies of some deputy of members of this House, sent to spy out their liberty, to misrepresent their actions, and to prey upon them,— men whose behavior, on many occasions, has caused the blood of those Sons of Liberty to recoil within them,—men promoted to the highest seats of justice: some, to my knowledge, were glad by going to foreign countries to escape being brought to a bar of justice in their own.

They protected by your arms? They have nobly taken up arms in your defence, have exerted their valor, amidst their constant and laborious industry, for the defence of a country whose frontiers, while drenched in blood, its interior parts have yielded all its little savings to your enlargement; and, believe me,—remember I this day told you so,—that the same spirit which actuated that people at first will continue with them still; but prudence forbids me to explain myself any further. God knows, I do not at this time speak from motives of party heat. What I deliver are the genuine sentiments of my heart; however superior to me in general knowledge and experience the respectable body of this House may be, yet I claim to know more of *America* than most of you, having seen and been conversant in that country. The people there are as truly loyal, I believe, as any subjects the king has; but a people jealous of their liberties, and who will vindicate them, if they should be violated. But the subject is too delicate. I will say no more.[12]

All of the eloquence in the world wouldn't have blocked the passage of the Stamp Act bill, for the votes to pass it had been bought and paid for in the usual manner well in advance of the "debate"; and except for Barré's splutterings it was, men said, a dull session. It was not the custom of the Commons to keep any record of debates, and we might never have heard of this effort had it not been for the presence in the gallery of a visitor from Connecticut, Jared Ingersoll, who jotted down his recollections of the speech and sent a copy of this to a newspaper in New London, which gladly printed it, 10 May 1765.

This Ingersoll was a promising young lawyer, and he might have been a mighty worker for the cause of independence if he had not, at this time, been steered the wrong way by no less a person than Benjamin Franklin, who was in London as agent for Pennsylvania. Franklin was very shrewd, politically, and he did not often make a mistake, but when he did, it was like this one, a whopper. He knew that it was the policy of the British cabinet to have native Americans act as stamp distributors, as far as they might be available, the idea being to forestall any talk of oppression from abroad. Franklin was no longer close to the American man in the street, and he did not realize how hot was the feeling against the Stamp Act in the colonies. He recommended to Ingersoll, and also to another friend, Richard Henry Lee of Virginia, that they get themselves distributor jobs and make a little easy money. Lee, who was at home, accepted the offer, but he was warned in time and hastily backed out, protesting that he hadn't meant it. This retreat saved his political life. He was one of *the* Lees; but if his name had become associated with that of the Stamp Act he would never again have been trusted by his fellow Virginians. As it was, he went on to become a leading Patriot. It was he who proposed in the Second Continental Congress the motion that was to become the basis of the Declaration of Independence.

Jared Ingersoll was not so fortunate. He was at sea when word got back to Connecticut that he had accepted a distributorship, and when he disembarked at New Haven he found a grim crowd awaiting him. Nobody actually laid a hand upon him, but the looks were daggers. He was escorted by armed men to Hartford, where he publicly resigned the office and promised not to do anything like that again. His captors repeatedly pointed out that his initials, J.I., were the same as those of a certain hateful character in the Bible, Judas Iscariot. This had absolutely nothing to do with the matter, but it was a powerful influence against him, and his enemy Naphtali Daggett, professor of divinity at Yale, was to make the most of it. Ingersoll was not allowed to be neutral, and a sudden lack of law business caused him to accept a royal judgeship, which confirmed his opponents in their suspicions and stamped him forever as a Loyalist.

Meanwhile, his letter to New London had been widely copied by other colonial newspapers, and the expression "Sons of Liberty" had been picked up and was being heard everywhere. "Independence" was scarcely mentioned in America at that time,[13] but "liberty" was. Sons of Liberty organizations began to spring up everywhere.

They were never nationally organized. There was no central committee. They did not send speakers to one another, and though they did correspond it was only intermittently and not on any schedule or with any expressed aim—at first. There was in fact something a little furtive about the Sons of Liberty, though they had no manner of passwords, secret handclasps, and all the rest, and they were never associated with Freemasonry. Members might be of the lower orders, especially in the cities, which was where they thrived, but there was usually one reputable lawyer, at least, behind each group, prepared to give it free advice but unwilling to permit the use of his name. The more flamboyant doings of the Sons were publicly deplored but privately applauded by those of the better sort.

What brought the colonies together, what made the

American Revolution possible, was the communications system set up by the so-called Committees of Correspondence. In general these came somewhat later than the Sons of Liberty, which sprang into being at the time of the passage of the Stamp Act, 1765; yet it is impossible to believe that the two were not somehow connected, the one leading to the other. The original Committee of Correspondence, it is usually conceded—and it was also, though not in name, one of the first Sons of Liberty organizations—was that little group of true believers that met once a week in the counting-room at the Chase & Speakman distillery in Hanover Square, Boston, to smoke their pipes and drink their flip and discuss the means of combatting tyranny. This group, of which Samuel Adams was the ringleader, and which was visited on one memorable occasion by his cousin John Adams, called itself, firmly, the Loyal Nine.

The Sons of Liberty were not illiterates—far from it! Though they did not have regular secretaries and did not exchange the scheduled dispatches that were to characterize the Committees of Correspondence a little later, they surely did keep in touch with one another somehow. Thus, when John Malcolm, a customs official who had marched against the Regulators in North Carolina, was transferred to New York, he was met by a committee of Sons who knew about his political leanings and served warning on him to abstain from putting them into action in his new job, and who, when he saw fit to ignore this warning, gave him a coat of hot tar. Thus, Zachariah Hood, appointed Stamp Act distributor for Maryland, who was hanged in effigy there, refused to resign, and skipped to New York; but he was called upon by a Sons of Liberty group in the latter colony, and made to resign after all. Thus, Ebenezer Richardson, a customs informer in Boston, chased by a handful of angry Patriots, took refuge in the house of a friend and in a mo-

ment of panic fired wildly out of a window, killing eleven-
year-old Christopher Sneider. Richardson was tried, found
guilty, but got a royal pardon. It would have been unwise
for Richardson to stay in Boston—the Sons had shown re-
straint when they spared him his life, and they could hardly
be expected to continue in this attitude after the pardon—
so he was transferred to Philadelphia. He was met on the
wharf in the City of Brotherly Love by Patriots who had
the tar already heated, and he escaped by the skin of his
teeth into a nearby wood, to be heard of in the customs
service no more.

Mobs were not new. Dublin, London, and cities on the
continent of Europe as well, in the eighteenth century had
many more mobs, and larger ones, nastier ones, than ever
did New York or Charleston or Boston town. The so-called
Gordon riots in London, launched in the name of a titled
Scottish bigot who had once called the Archbishop of
Canterbury the Whore of Babylon, lasted for eight days,
smashed Newgate Prison, releasing all the prisoners, almost
took over the Bank of England, damaged or tore down completely about 100 houses, worth more than £100,000, and
caused the death of 285 persons, the wounding of 173 more,
as a result of which 450 persons were arrested, 25 of whom
were hanged.[14] Nothing even remotely like the Gordon Riots
occurred in America. American mobs, much smaller, were
more personalized, more direct, and *single-purposed*. They
never displayed an indiscriminate savagery. When they had
done what they set out to do they were dissolved in good
order, quietly. The most famous of them was the Boston
Tea Party, in which 342 chests of tea, worth £18,000 at
wholesale prices, were methodically dumped into the harbor. The only *unplanned* damage of the Boston Tea Party
was done to a padlock that happened to be the personal
property of the skipper of one of the three violated vessels;

In John Trumbull's mock epic M'Fingal, *the Tory hero gets rough treatment at the Liberty Pole* (left) *and then, tarred and feathered, is toted through the streets* (right).

and this was an accident, for which the rioters apologized when they replaced the lock.

The Sons of Liberty sometimes were dubbed by the Tories the Sons of Licentiousness, a name that never really caught on, or sometimes, more simply, the Cudgel Boys; but in fact they did not often resort to violence, though they were quick to threaten it. The unspoken word, the meaningful look: these were their favorite weapons. The man whose windows had been broken—glass was expensive, panes small —would think twice before he cheered the Parliament in public again. The man who saw a likeness of himself dangling from a Liberty Pole, with a placard around his neck to identify it (for the makers of effigies were not convincing artists), inevitably began to wonder what it would feel like if that had been he, himself, rather than just a stuffed figure; and this thought did not make for ease and comfort.

What was sometimes euphemistically known as night soil often came into play. The word "merchants" meant not only importers and exporters but also retail dealers, and any man who had a shop and who refused to heed the warnings of the local Sons of Liberty might wake one day to find that the windows of the said shop had been bedaubed with human faeces. The product was easily obtained. Every house and every shop had a privy, or jakes, which was usually outside, in the backyard. The cleaning-off would take a long time, and it was unpleasant work, in the course of which the word would go around that So-and-so must be selling English goods, for the Sons of Liberty had paid him a visit; and this, of course, was bad for business.

It must be remembered that there was no police department to apply to. That institution had not yet come into existence. Call out the militia? By the time the first drum roll had been sounded the house would have been burned to the ground, the crowd dispersed, and nobody would know anything. As for the county authorities: as Sheriff Greenleaf of Boston once complained, when asked to do something about a series of disorders there, where could he find deputies, when they were all running with the mob?

The worst threat was that of tar-and-feathering.

Feathers always seem frivolous, and perhaps this is the reason why this torment has loomed before a later generation as something ludicrous, an act of horseplay, hoydenish perhaps but essentially a harmless pastime, a vulgar display of spirits. In truth there was nothing funny about it. The feathers were mere decoration, an afterthought, and could be dispensed with. The tar it was that told the tale—a tale of unabashed cruelty, mankind at its lowest.

This beastly business was not new, nor had it always been extra-legal. The first record of it is dated 1191, when Richard I of England (the Lion-Heart) was making preparations for a crusade to the Holy Land. He would go by sea, because of the situation on the continent of Europe, and he had amassed at various English ports enormous supplies of beans, cheese, and salt pork, besides ten thousand horseshoes, in addition to those already on the horses. His instructions to his fighting men, who it might be feared would wax restless on such a long trip, were specific, including as they did such provisions that if one man murdered another he should be lashed to the corpse and then thrown overboard; also: ". . . item, a thief or felon that hath stolen, being lawfully convicted, shal have his head shorne, and boyling pitch poured upon his head, and feathers or downe strawed upon same, whereby he may be knowen, and so at the first landing-place they shall come to, there to be cast up."

There was a Sons of Liberty system in just about every seacoast town and county, though not all of them had that very name. Seldom indeed were they regularly organized, with bylaws, with elected leaders. More often they were only mobs thrown together for an occasion. But—they were *there*. Like a modern navy they existed not so much for the harm they could do, or the protection that they could afford, as for the threat they posed. The very fact that their members and even their captains remained anonymous made them the more terrible in the popular imagination. Like the later Ku Klux Klan, the members of the Sons of Liberty preferred to work in secret, shrouding their movements, changing their personnel. In some places they had slightly different names, local names, though they were always known generically as the Sons. And tar was their most terrible weapon. Nobody who had ever seen a man treated with it was likely to forget.

Pine tar ordinarily was used, a stickier, sharper substance than beech tar or the various kinds of coal tar. It was heated before the victim, so that he might see in its sulfurous bubblings the pain that would soon be his. This is significant. In medieval days and even in the time of the Renaissance it was the practice in most prisons to show a suspected man the instruments of torture, either one by one or all together, so that he might reflect upon these before the actual process of scream-inducement began. He could of course change his mind. He could confess. Even as late as Elizabethan days in merrie England, when only one form of physical torture was permitted, the rack, and that only in certain circumstances, and by order of certain high officials, the law itself insisted upon such a display. The use of each wheel and crank and line and pulley would be explained to the prisoner, so that he knew in advance just how he would feel when they were tearing him oh-so-slowly apart. Then he would be taken back to his cell to think it over.

The reason for this, its justification in the eyes of its practitioners, was the confession that might well expose a plot against the state or against the lives of certain statesmen. Torture was used only in treason cases, and then only after elaborate preliminaries and certain safeguards such as a physician's examination of the heart of the intended victim.

No such pretense at justification existed in the instance of colonial American tar-and-feathering. No confession was sought. The deed to be done was savagery of a sort that would have shamed the Mohawks themselves. Hence, the presence of the victim while the tar was being heated, leading to no new evidence, could only be attributed to *Schadenfreude*—delight in the suffering of others.

The wretch was stripped to the waist, or sometimes stripped naked. A ladle with a long handle was used, and the hissing, spitting stuff was poured over his shoulders, his chest, his back. A little of it, or much, might be emptied upon the top of his head, which could cause him to be blinded in one or both eyes: this had happened. If his breeches had been ripped off, and his underpants, a ladleful might be dumped upon his genitals, rendering him, as likely as not, impotent for the rest of his life.

If the victim was but to be dropped into a ditch, for his friends to rescue later, then feathers might be thought to be wasted on him; but if he was to be mounted on a rail, one leg on each side, to be toted through the streets, the carriers joggling it furiously so that the poor man felt as though he was being split in half, *then* feathers—or for lack of feathers, ashes or ripped-up cloths—were copiously applied, for the crowds loved them and would hurrah.

Getting the stuff off was the most painful part of the business. For all the oil that was used, skin would come off with the tar; and days, even weeks, were needed to finish the task, though in a larger sense the victim of a tar-and-feathering never did completely recover.

The practice was not common, and it seems to have been confined to the New England provinces at one end of the colonial line, and the provinces of the Deep South—the Carolinas and Georgia—at the other. The middle provinces, for the most part, abstained.

The *threat*, however, always was there. And the threat was usually enough. A man who for whatever reason had made himself unpopular might have a ball of cold tar encased in a fluff of feathers slipped into his hand in some public place or sent to him by some innocent messenger. He would understand; and he would move away.

The case of John Mein illustrates this point. He was a stouthearted Scot who moved to Boston just after the French and Indian War, and there, in partnership with one Fleeming, he ran a bookshop and a weekly newspaper, the *Chronicle*. In addition, Mein started the first circulating library in America, and at one time he was said to have had ten thousand volumes on his shelves.

The *Chronicle* was kept carefully neutral for several years; but Mein, after a while, seemingly against the advice of his partner, began to take the side of the royal government by showing up some of the Patriots' shabbier tricks. He was warned; but he snorted defiance. Samuel Adams himself publicly abjured him to cease "this opposition to an awakened, an enlightened, and determined continent," but he continued in the columns of the *Chronicle* to urge the local merchants to break their nonimportation agreements. His office was picketed, one of the men carrying a sign that read "Mean is the Man; M____n is his name." He himself was attacked on King Street in broad daylight, but escaped. His windows were broken. A group of the less responsible citizens, 28 October 1769, tarred a man accused of informing on a smuggler, and they paraded this poor devil through the streets for three hours, stopping him for a long while before the Mein and Fleeming plant, so that Mr. Mein could get a good look. Afterward Mein was handed the chunk of cold tar, the feathers. He left the colony by the next ship.

4

The Curious Case of Benjamin Church

Each side in what both sides liked to refer to as "this unnatural contest" coddled its physicians. Teachers and preachers, lawyers as well, editors too, were variously treated, depending upon their respective political opinions. Such men would be execrated by one side, fondled by the other. A professional person with a Patriot background, for instance, might find it hard to make a living in a city held by the British, as Boston was in the beginning, as Charleston and Philadelphia were to be a good part of the time, and New York virtually throughout the war. By the same token, Tory practitioners were so severely discouraged at home by their Loyalist neighbors that they were driven to take refuge behind the enemy's lines. Their skill, their ability, and experience had nothing to do with the matter. It was their opinion about independence that counted.

The physicians made up an exception. A medical man as the American Revolution was forming could choose either side he wished, and he would be tolerated and even backed by members of the other side.

The reasons for this was that there were so few of them.

They were needed by Patriots and Tories alike. They were so badly needed that they were even permitted neutrality, something denied to everybody else.

The only American physician of the time of whom it could be said that he had an international reputation was Dr. Benjamin Rush, surgeon-general of the Continental Army, a delegate to the Second Continental Congress, a signer of the Declaration of Independence. He was a pioneer in the study of tooth decay, a chemist, an early psychiatrist, who established the first free medical dispensary in America. He was perhaps best known in his heyday, however, as the man who had put forth in a learned paper the absurd theory that the rum ration dealt out to the troops not only did them no good but just conceivably could have been detrimental to their health. He had written this in his capacity as surgeon-general, and nothing, of course, had come of it, for everybody knew that men needed periodical jolts of rum or some other alcoholic drink in order to keep up their strength. It is a proof of Rush's prestige that in spite of this ridiculous assertion and in spite too of the fact that he did not think George Washington was up to his job and believed that he should be replaced by somebody with more military experience—Gates, say—Dr. Benjamin Rush continued to be the most popular practitioner and teacher in Philadelphia.

Earlier in the contest, and in fact even before the shooting had started, two of the most active Patriots were physicians. One was to wear a martyr's crown in history, whilst the other was to be relegated to the pit Abaddon guards, a pariah never to be recalled.

Joseph Warren was one of the more eligible bachelors of Boston—young, slight, dapper, with an amiable disposition and a very remunerative practice. A Harvard man, he was fond of bright waistcoats. But he was not a mere ornament on patriotism's mantelshelf! He was a hard worker, always ready to give a stirring speech, a committeeman, a presenter of resolutions. Though the British surely knew of his political proclivities,[15] he went right on serving his country, as he saw it. It was Dr. Warren who sent out his friend Paul Revere, the silversmith, the night of 18 April 1775 to warn the people of Concord that the British were coming. (He sent out another messenger, William Dawes, Jr., at the same time; and Dawes rode farther and awakened more Patriots than did Revere, who was captured by the British so that he never did get to Concord, as Dawes did; but the poet Longfellow seems not to have heard of William Dawes, Jr.)

When John Hancock and the two Adamses, Samuel and John, went to Philadelphia as delegates to the Second Continental Congress, Dr. Warren became acting chairman of the Boston committee of safety. The newly formed provincial congress offered him a commission as major general of the Massachusetts militia, and he accepted. The very next day was the day of Bunker Hill, and Dr. Warren, no man to hide from trouble, went out to the tip of the Charlestown peninsula on foot long after it had become obvious that the garrison there was doomed. General Putnam on Bu. ker Hill and Colonel Prescott on Breed's Hill, where all the fighting was, successively offered him the command, which he declined. Whether he did this out of modesty—for he had no military experience—or whether he did it because he was not yet *actually* a major general, not having the commission itself but only a notification that he was about to *be* commissioned: this we will never know, nor does it matter. He never came out of that redoubt alive. He was thirty-four years old. He was buried in a mass grave with the others, and there his corpse remained for nine months until the British had evacuated Boston, when it was dug up and identified by Paul Revere himself by means of two false teeth Revere had made for his friend. It is believed that this is the first time a body was identified in this fashion, though the practice is routine today.

Dr. Benjamin Church was quite a different person. He was bland of manner, self-assured. Like Warren he fancied himself as a spread-eagle orator, and when he gave the annual Massacre Day memorial speech in 1773 the Old South was packed to the last inch of standing room. But he could be practical too. He was a member of the Massachusetts provincial council and also of the Boston committee of safety, and from time to time he had served on many lesser committees, serving notices, investigating conditions, making complaints, all in the Patriot cause. He was one of those appointed to receive George Washington officially and formally under the big elm at Cambridge when Washington came to take command of the just-authorized Continental Army. He was in almost everything, and knew everybody. He wrote, too. He wrote scorching editorials in the local papers, and his poetry as well was published.

Benjamin Church, another graduate of Harvard, had studied also in the London Medical College, and he had brought home with him an English wife. There were whispers that he was not doing right by her, that he was inclined to cut up on the side, the sly dog; but nobody doubted the value of his services to the cause. When the Adamses, second cousins, had gone to Philadelphia, along with John Hancock, and Dr. Warren had been slain on Breed's Hill, then was Benjamin Church hailed as the Number One Patriot in those parts.

The provincial council appointed him a committee of one to carry to the Congress at Philadelphia a request that a Continental Army be authorized, and the Congress not only did this but expressed its faith in the messenger by ap-

Benjamin Church

pointing him director of the new army's whole hospital system. He was thus the nation's first surgeon-general, serving before Benjamin Rush.

Dr. Church wrote a letter. It was written in cipher, and one of the many mysteries about it was the person to whom it was addressed. The good doctor declared that this was his brother-in-law, John Fleeming, the Boston printer, partner until lately of John Mein, who at the not-at-all-veiled threat of the Sons of Liberty had skipped the land. Fleeming himself was deemed a Tory; at least, he lingered in Boston, where now the Tories from all over New England were congregating.

Dr. Church gave this letter to a woman, a friend of his, who lived in Cambridge. He instructed her to get it to somebody else, who would see that it was taken or sent into the city; for, as the siege became more businesslike, getting things into and out of Boston, across the Neck, had become a chancy task. Church believed that he could trust this woman. He had known her for some time, and in fact had been keeping her. (The rumors were right.)

The woman was about to go to Newport, Rhode Island. If you didn't think that you could smuggle a letter across the Neck you sent it to Newport, where it was given to Captain Wallace of H.M.S. *Rose*, who would see that it got to Boston, for the Royal Navy had complete control not only of the high seas in that part of the world but also of the coastal waters of New England.

Captain Wallace could not be found, and the woman, who perhaps was not very bright, before she returned to Cambridge gave the letter to a friend, a man named Wainwood. Wainwood too failed to find Captain Wallace, and he conferred with a friend of *his*, a fellow Whig, named Maxwell. They opened the letter; but when they learned that it was written in cipher they went no further—for the present.

A few days later Wainwood got a letter from the woman in Cambridge. Why had the letter not been delivered? Wainwood and Maxwell put their heads together over this. How did *she* know that it hadn't been delivered? She must have been in touch with somebody in Boston. That looked suspicious. They took the letter to Henry Ward, a Providence Whig, and *he* took it to the head of the Rhode Island militia, Brigadier General Nathanael Greene; and the fat was in the fire.

Greene was a self-educated blacksmith, a Quaker who had been read out of the Friends' meeting because of his military activities. He was too young to have seen service in the French and Indian War, and his experience was confined to the parade ground, but he was a natural soldier and was to prove one of Washington's best generals. Now he went to Washington's headquarters at Cambridge, with the letter, and he picked up the woman on his way.

It might seem odd to a modern military man that the commander-in-chief should take over the questioning of such a prisoner in person; but it must be remembered that this was a brand-new army, and there was not as yet any manner of intelligence department in it. It is hard to think of the tall handsome courtly stiff George Washington as an iron-jawed interrogator; but he did the job, and well. The woman held out for some hours, but at last she broke down and confessed that it was Dr. Church who had given her the letter.

The letter itself meanwhile had been turned over to a couple of amateur cryptographers, one a Congregational minister, the other a retired militia colonel. They examined it separately and came in with similar reports. The letter, they believed, had been meant for General Gage. It contained a vast amount of incorrect figures on the artillery pieces and other military stores amassed by the Patriots in Massachusetts, Connecticut, Rhode Island, and New Hampshire.

Church's desk was impounded, but somebody else had got there first, and the papers, such as remained, were helter-skelter. Then Church himself appeared, and he was arrested.

He readily acknowledged the authorship of the letter. Yes, he admitted, he had hoped that it would get to General Gage. He, the writer, had deliberately exaggerated the extent of the Patriot preparations and the amount of their accumulated supplies. He had done this, he said, in the hope of frightening the British into making a peace offer. It was peace he sought. He was thinking of his country all the time.

Washington called a council of his chief staff officers, but they found, to their dismay, that there was no charge upon which they could try Dr. Church. The articles of war under which the new army was operating—the ink was scarcely dry upon them—had not foreseen the possibility of such a crime as corresponding with the enemy. This would be corrected, of course. Meanwhile the prisoner was turned over to the Continental Congress, which, after a while, turned him over to the Massachusetts provincial congress, which, November 2, "utterly expelled" him.

Church defended himself, and vehemently. He might have been indiscreet, he protested, but he never was treasonous. The authorities did not believe him.

News of the secret had leaked out, and public indignation ran high. It was feared that if Dr. Church were jailed in or anywhere near Cambridge the jail would be broken by a mob and the prisoner lynched. So he was sent, instead, to Norwich, Connecticut, where he was ordered to be confined without reading matter, without writing materials, and without any visitors.

After several years of this—the siege of Boston long since had been lifted—he was permitted, on his plea of poor health, to live at home, though under strict house arrest. Later still—the war was nearing its end by this time—he was permitted to go aboard a "small schooner" as a passenger to the West Indies. That schooner never did get to the islands. In fact, it never was seen or heard of again.

Dr. Church's widow went to England, where the government granted her a pension of £150 a year. She did not specify in her application what these payments might be for; but she did say, significantly, that General Gage, in retirement, would know.

Benjamin Church never was convicted of anything. Indeed, he never was charged with anything. His existence throughout the latter part of his life embarrassed the authorities. Yet no one stood up to shout that he'd been dealt an injustice. Everybody believed in his guilt. He was known to have visited Boston 22 April 1775, just a few days after the Lexington-Concord running fight, and many weeks before Bunker Hill, when his excuse was that he wished to visit some patients; and he was seen on this occasion coming out of Province House, the official home of the governor, Thomas Gage, who certainly was not a patient. Nobody doubted that Dr. Church had been feeding military information to the governor from that time until his arrest, and that he had been duly paid. When he disappeared, therefore, unless it was his widow, nobody wept.

Publication of the Gage papers only a few years ago confirmed the unofficial damnation. Church had indeed written many letters to General Gage, who had a large slush fund from which to take care of his spies. As early as

May 13, more than a month before the battle, he had warned the general that the Patriots planned to fortify Bunker's Hill. Moreover, it had been Church—though he might not have been alone in this—who told the British in Boston that the Patriots were amassing military supplies in the inland town of Concord, the spark that set off the Revolution.

The arrest of the first surgeon-general shocked the Patriots, and caused them to look at one another askance, asking themselves whom after all could they trust? Church was immediately put down as a Tory of the deepest dye, the very epitome of treason pretending to be a Patriot, until the emergence of Benedict Arnold the worst Loyalist of them all. But Church was not a Loyalist. He did not act from any political principle, but only because he needed money. He was not a traitor to any ideal. He had let his women get out of hand—there is reason to believe that the one who carried the message to Newport, and whose name was never made public, was not his only mistress—and so he sold secrets. His was a sad case. All things considered, it was just as well for him and for everybody else that he got lost.

5

No Splash in the Sewer

IT NEVER FAILS to amuse Americans when they hear Europeans use "the United States" as a plural noun: "The United States are—" It sounds naive. It used to infuriate Theodore Roosevelt when he was President and "the United States are" was common usage in official correspondence with other nations; and he tried, vainly, to bully those other nations into using the name as a singular: "the United States *is*." This of course is the way every American thinks of it, for he considers his country one thing, an entity, rather than a casual agglomeration of sovereignties.

It was not always so.

From the beginning, the colonies, whenever they got near enough, had snarled at one another. Though there were spots like the Dutch of New York, the Swedes of New Jersey, the Highland Scots in upper New York State and in North Carolina, and the sundry Germanic groups that had settled in Pennsylvania, the colonies were, for all practical purposes, ethnically at one. They spoke the same language. Their founders, and *their* forebears, had known the same middle-class background. They worked hard for what they got, and expected to go on working. The class differences among them were so small as to be negligible; and there were not as yet any vast inherited fortunes, not any dynasties.

The colonists' political problems were different, for they had different types of colonial government. Some were family properties; some operated under royal charters; a few—Connecticut and Rhode Island—were virtually self-governing.

It might be thought that they all faced the same Indian menace, and that this would bring them together. But the Indians too were a changing people, one thing here, another there, never stable.

Communication among the colonies was difficult. There were virtually no roads, and amazingly little coastwise passenger travel, perhaps because the vessels were so uncomfortable. River traffic was no more than a dribble.

There was not even any *district* companionability. New Englanders got along tolerably well with one another, though they were a notably cantankerous, quarrelsome lot, having frequent recourse to the law; but New Englanders and New Yorkers, though placed side by side in the geographical scheme of things, drove one another wild. New England was four colonies then. Maine, virtually uninhabited, was a part of Massachusetts, and Vermont, known as the New Hampshire Grants, was a district in dispute between New Hampshire and New York: the fight over these claims was one of the "little wars" that antedated the Revolution and went along with it as well.

Virginia and Pennsylvania because of clashing claims to western lands on several occasions verged upon a shooting war, and so did Connecticut and Pennsylvania, who both wanted the Wyoming Valley, now a part of Pennsylvania.

The New Englanders, the Yankees, indeed, were loved by none on their side of the sea. Pennsylvanians, smug, sure of themselves, from their glittering metropolis of Philadelphia looked down upon them and sneered at them as graceless, gawky; while the New Englanders' holier-than-thou manners, their too-obvious belief that they were the chosen of God, made them universally disliked. Virginians and the quasi-aristocrats of Maryland shook their heads and clucked their tongues at the "levelling," that dangerous tendency that seemed to be accepted by the Yankees, who were sometimes referred to as "the Wise Men of the East."

Nevertheless, from the earliest days there had been far-seeing Americans who looked toward a union. In 1698 William Penn himself had proposed such an association. His idea was that two representatives of each colony should meet once a year "as near as conveniently may be to the most central colony for ease of the delegates," or oftener in time of war, but at least once in every two years even in peacetime. These meetings should be called by and should be presided over by a high commissioner appointed by the Crown, an official who in time of war should command the colonial forces. Nothing came of this suggestion.

There were other union plans proposed in 1684, 1694, 1711, 1722, 1744, and 1748, some of them at conventions that took place in New London, Boston, Lancaster, and Albany. These conventions in general were concerned with more immediate and more parochial problems, and when they did consider the possibility of a union of the colonies it was usually just in order to tut-tut Mr. Penn's choice of Philadelphia as the meeting place for a master colonial council. The great Quaker had not actually stipulated that the City of Brotherly Love be used for this purpose, but he had strongly implied his belief that it should; and the other colonies did not agree. But though there was some talk, nothing was done.

It was not until 1754 that a really responsible convention took the matter up at least semi-seriously.

This convention was called at the request of the Crown in order to make more clear and specific the understanding between the coastal colonists and the Iroquois Indians, the great Six Nations confederacy. War with France once again was about to break out, and London wanted to be certain of where those sixteen thousand armed redskins stood. This, naturally, did not interest the southern colonies. The convention held in Albany from 19 June to 10 July was attended by twenty-five commissioners from only seven colonies—Massachusetts, New Hampshire, Rhode Island, Connecticut, Pennsylvania, Maryland, and New York.

Like all conferences with Indians this convention consisted of a great deal of orotund oratory, ughing, pipe-smoking, and eating and drinking, all of which the Indians considered their due. Eventually an agreement was reached.

Meanwhile two members of a special committee appointed to study the possibility of closer cooperation among the colonies had brought in a report that was largely the work of two of its members—easily the two most eminent delegates to the convention—Benjamin Franklin of Pennsylvania and Thomas Hutchinson of Massachusetts. This report was nothing less than a full-length formal proposal for a union of the colonies.

The authors of this plan intended to erect a public authority as obligatory in its sphere as the local governments were in their spheres. This would have been not a mere league, but a self-sustaining government. The credit of this conception is due to the illustrious Franklin. It was original and American. It was comprehensive and grand. It is not strange that the form devised to carry it out should have been imperfect. The time had not ripened, the way had not been opened, for such a stride in political science as a worthy embodiment of this ideal would have been. It required the discipline and experience of the succeeding thirty years, the growth of a public opinion for a union, the rise of a sentiment of nationality, the possession of sovereignty, long training of the general mind in politics, and the wisdom of a cluster of the peers of Franklin in intellect, before the conception could be embodied in a worthy form. Divine Providence permitted Franklin to share in the experience, to aid in forming the more perfect Union of the Constitution, and to see his countrymen establish it as the law of the land.[16]

All of the colonies, excepting only Georgia and Nova Scotia, it stipulated, should be united under a president-general appointed by and removable by the Crown. There should be between two and seven delegates from each colony, the number depending upon the colony's contribution to the general treasury. There should be in full. council forty-eight delegates, twenty-five of whom would form a quorum, "among whom there shall be one or more from a majority of the Colonies," arranged thus: Massachusetts Bay seven, New Hampshire two, Connecticut five, Rhode Island two, New York four, New Jersey three, Pennsylvania six, Maryland four, Virginia seven, North Carolina four, South Carolina four.[17] These delegates should decide, themselves, each year, where the capital should be. It was all carefully worked out. But it got very little attention at Albany. The convention accepted it almost without discussion, but every one of the seven colonies represented at the convention turned down the plan through its colonial legislature even before word of it could reach London, so that the world was never to learn Whitehall's opinion of it, much less the Crown's. And that was the end of that. A pity. The plan was a good one, and deserved more attention than it got.

"Independence" as yet was unthinkable. "Liberty," however, was often on American tongues, and perhaps even more often in American minds. That Parliament would seek to impose taxes upon the colonists without any preliminary consultation with them, as Parliament seemed intent upon doing, chafed the Patriots.

A later generation was to favor the cry of "No taxation without representation," which was somewhat too cumbersome to be used as a slogan in the field. Nevertheless, men's minds in America *were* turning to the problem of representation, in some form or other. Various plans were suggested, though none was seriously put forward by a responsible party. The difficulties would be enormous. Prices in London were known to be scandalously high, so that only a very rich American could have afforded to take a seat in the House of Commons after a long and expensive sea voyage. There were not many rich Americans. Besides, any such delegation would be lost, crowded into a corner, impotent; or else it would be swiftly corrupted. Americans who had visited England and watched the system at work harbored no illusions about their countrymen staunchly withstanding the evils of the system. Parliament just at that time was showing at its worst, its lowest. Bribery was an accepted and widespread practice. The bribes were not necessarily in cash. Titles were more often used, and pensions, and sinecures. Americans, no matter how carefully selected, could make no splash in that sewer.

Men did give thought to the *possibility*, however, since anything less might be esteemed disloyal. In 1770 a pamphlet published in Philadelphia—anonymously, as was so often the case in those days—proposed a plan of proportional representation in all the American colonies *and* Ireland. This pamphlet had a big sale, and caused a great deal of talk. It proposed, also, the creation of ten American peers. Nothing came of it.

In 1774 the distinguished financier Thomas Wharton, in that same city, came out with a somewhat similar suggestion, which he put forward for the benefit of the forthcoming First Continental Congress. It got scant study at that convention, however, for a fellow Philadelphian, who was also a delegate, Joseph Galloway, had a plan of his own, which drew all eyes and ears.

Galloway was accustomed to such attention. He might have been born on a platform, speechifying even before he started to bawl.

With a perspicacity not always to be noted in him, he warned the Continental Congress that the colonies must compromise or have war; and war, he averred, would mean one of three things:

1. a taking-over by Great Britain and a long and painful military occupation;

2. or, Independence for a short time, to be terminated whenever some European power decided to gulp this tempting tidbit;

3. or, Independence for a slightly longer period, to be followed by a debilitating civil war between North and South, which would be "won" by the North.

The proceedings of the First Continental Congress, like those of the Stamp Act Congress that had preceded it, and like those of the Second Continental Congress that was to follow it, were secret. Non-delegates were not admitted to any meeting, and the tally of votes never was published. John Dickinson, largely through the influence of Galloway, had not been elected to this congress at the time the plan of union was proposed, though he was to *be* elected soon afterward; but he was a hard man to keep a political secret from, and undoubtedly he knew what was going on inside the hall almost as soon as it happened.

These two were enemies. They had differed, loudly, on the question of whether Pennsylvania should continue under the proprietorship of the Penn family or should apply for a royal charter; and they had never been able to stand one another since. Yet they had many things in common, and if they had been able to get together they might have changed the course of history.

They were about the same age: Dickinson had been born in 1732, Galloway in 1731. Each came from a propertied family in Maryland but was professionally quartered in Philadelphia. Each had married money and was a successful lawyer. Each was considered conservative and feared the effect of Yankee "levelling."

They were different in *manner*, and perhaps this was the explanation of the rift; perhaps it was a matter of personality, personal irritation. Galloway was positive, not to say pugnacious. Dickinson was a seemingly meek man, though insistent, stubborn, and at one time he so far lost control of himself as to issue a challenge.[18] This challenge Galloway refused to accept, which is a pity, for such an encounter—between two men so closely associated with Quakerism—surely would have been unique in the annals of the code duello.

Galloway, a specialist in deeds, titles, wills, who had been speaker of the Pennsylvania Assembly for many years, fancied himself as an orator. Dickinson rarely raised his voice, but he could write like an angel, and long before the title was bestowed upon Thomas Jefferson he was known as the Penman of the Revolution. He wrote many intelligent, well-received pamphlets on the colonial situation, but his *Letters of a Pennsylvania Farmer* was acclaimed as a masterpiece. It was a closely reasoned, beautifully set forth exposition of the emergent liberalism in America, though nowhere in it do the words "independence" or "separation" appear.

When the situation became taut, and men in public life were forced to flop one way or the other, Dickinson for a long while hovered like an uncertain kite. Yet he continued to enjoy the respect of both sides, which was most unusual. He was to be a member of the Second Continental Congress, yet even when the Pennsylvania delegation had voted for the Declaration of Independence—the unit rule was in effect —he found himself unable to sign the thing. He did serve the new republic, however. He was a brigadier general of militia, though he saw no action. He was a governor of the new state of Delaware. He was a founder of Dickinson College, which was named for him. But he is best known in history as the author of *Letters of a Pennsylvania Farmer.*

Galloway, though he lacked the lustre that penmanship conferred, possessed something else denied to his rival, the close friendship of the grand old man of Pennsylvania politics, Benjamin Franklin, who was presently in London as Pennsylvania's agent. Franklin had been shocked by what he saw in the unhallowed halls of Parliament, and had written home to caution friends against any plan to institute colonial representation in the House of Commons—or, for that matter, in the Lords. That way, he warned, lay submergence.

Galloway might have had this warning in mind when he proposed to the First Continental Congress, in 1774, his elaborate Plan of Union. He probably conceived of it as a compromise, a dam lifted against the onrush of republican ideas, particularly those from New England.

The plan provided for the establishment of a Grand Council of the American mainland colonies, to be chosen triennially by the several provincial legislatures, which themselves were to remain unchanged: the plan provided that "each Colony shall retain its present Constitution and powers of regulating and governing its own internal Police in all Cases whatsoever." A president-general appointed by the King during pleasure would preside over the council. Any piece of legislation that concerned the colonies might, under this plan, "originate and be formed and digested" in either Parliament or the Grand Council, though the enactments of that council would be subject to the approval of both Parliament and the King. The council, as Galloway was careful to point out, would be "an inferior and distinct branch of the British legislature."

It was a good plan, and he had worked it out well, but it came too late. The Congress, having considered it, turned it down, six to five, voting en bloc by colonies.

Galloway did not take his defeat gracefully. An impatient man, short of temper, accustomed to getting his own way, he believed that he had done all he could do toward rescuing the infatuated colonies that were on the very verge of disaster, or, as he himself somewhat confusingly put it, "we are on the brink of a Precipice big with the fate of America." [19] He openly went over to the Loyalists.

When General Howe started across New Jersey, Galloway left his property (which he valued at £40,000) behind and joined the British in the field. He made himself useful around Howe's headquarters as an authority on the rebels, and after Philadelphia had been captured he became *very* useful, being appointed Superintendent of Civil Administration—in other words, non-military boss of the largest and most important city in America, not to mention the surrounding countryside. When, after a comfortable winter there, while the Continental troops were suffering at Valley Forge, the British cleared out by land for New York, Joseph Galloway went along with them. He did not seem to be short of funds. He remained only a little while in New York, then went to London, where he set himself up as an expert in American affairs.

He was not made much of, in England. Distinguished exiles from the colonies by this time cluttered the drawing rooms and coffeehouses of London, Bristol too, and Bath. Galloway lacked personal charm, and though he had money he had few friends. His mentor Franklin, whose usefulness as a colonial agent had ceased with the Hutchinson letters scandal, one of Samuel Adams's greatest triumphs, had returned to America; and these two never did meet again. Galloway was presented to the King. He was consulted from time to time by Lord North and other bigwigs. He clung to his belief that the colonies could be saved for the Crown if only Englishmen went about it the right way—that is, Joseph Galloway's way. He was always ready to produce interesting figures. For instance, he asserted that there had been 6,057 houses in Philadelphia when Howe took over that city, and of these only 597 had been deserted by Patriots, from which he deduced that nine-tenths of the city was loyal. Later, by means of some method known only to sociologists, he modified this figure to four-fifths. The news caused no stir.

If his Plan of Union had been adopted, Joseph Galloway kept saying in England, there would be no war. Nevertheless, he framed another such plan, updating the first, and then another, and another . . . Each of these was formally presented to the government for consideration, and its receipt formally acknowledged. One of them, some said, actually reached the King, who glanced at it. But nothing was done.

Late in the war there was a Parliamentary investigation of the conduct in America of the Howe brothers, general and admiral, and Joseph Galloway was called to testify as a matter of course. He swore, among other things, that at the outbreak of hostilities four-fifths of the American people were loyal, though he never did say how he came by this figure.

He lived on, forgotten by both sides. In 1793 he petitioned the Executive Council of Pennsylvania for permission to return to his native land, but the petition was rejected without comment. He died in England in September of 1803, at the age of seventy-three.

6

The War Moves South

A REVOLUTION HAS BEEN DEFINED as an unlawful change in the conditions of lawfulness. The American colonists were a conservative people, and it was some time after the outbreak of hostilities before they ventured, gingerly, into the giddy whirl of expropriation.

Not that there was anything wrong, to contemporary thinking, about the seizure of a traitor's property. It had always been done; and the assumption was that it always would be. Each side in the American Revolution, of course, deemed the other side traitorous; but the Patriots held most of the country; the Loyalist forces, together with the Hessians and the redcoats, controlled only such ground around them as their muskets could command—somewhat less than a hundred yards.

Revolutions traditionally concern themselves with the redistribution of vast landholdings, with the breaking up of estates. This was to happen in America, but only on a small scale, a non-revolutionary scale. Not that there was no land hunger! but the average American coveted not his neighbor's fields but rather the rolling seas of acreage beyond the mountains, property he probably never would see, but could dream of and invest in.

The kings of England and those of France, though not the kings of Spain, in the early days had seen fit to bestow huge chunks of American real estate upon any courtiers who had kowtowed to the Throne with sufficient fervor. Men could and did own millions of acres across the sea. But this practice soon ceased, and the huge grants, unexploited, were broken up, or crumbled of themselves.

Lord Granville at one time owned about a third of North Carolina, but this holding became history. The Virginia property of Lord Fairfax, the property young George Washington had helped to survey, at its tops ran to some six million acres, but it was not held together for a long time. When the Revolution came, the Van Rensselaer manor along the Hudson River in New York probably was the largest piece of privately owned land in the colonies. In shape roughly a rectangle, it measured twenty-four by twenty-eight miles, which made it two-thirds the size of Rhode Island. The Patriots never laid hands on any part of it.

This was not the case elsewhere in New York. Long Island, Staten Island, and Manhattan were in British hands almost continuously throughout the war, but there was still plenty of land upstate, land from which the Tory owners had fled to the safety of the city, and it has been estimated that estates to the total value of $3,600,000, a staggering sum, were confiscated.

Expropriation was not a one-party punishment. The Tories too took over whenever they had a chance, usually in a city.[20]

In the beginning, confiscation of property was not resorted to and seldom even threatened. The earliest Loyalists were simply shunned, or sometimes hooted at or spat upon. Later they submitted or refused to submit to what a subsequent generation would name a boycott. They might be deprived of their right to carry on their businesses or to exercise their professions—unless they were physicians, who were always welcome by both sides, no matter what their politics might be. Not until toward the middle of the war, when it became evident that this would be a long struggle, did the various new state governments look upon the deserted houses and untilled fields with an envious eye, calculating mentally what they would bring if sold in public. Then suits were filed, and notices served, while commissioners of sequestration and commissioners of forfeiture sprang up all over the land.

There were of course families that were split, as there were to be families that deliberately, as it were, split themselves. That is, the head of the family, before lighting out for Tory-held territory and the service of the King, would make over the title to the whole property to some son or nephew who, whatever his personal views might be, was instructed to stay home and when questioned to pronounce himself a Patriot. Thus, whichever side won, the land would stay in the family. There was nothing new about this dodge. It had been resorted to repeatedly by Scottish families, especially in the Highlands, in the Jacobite uprisings of 1715 and 1745. It was seldom successful.

There were shifts of ownership, then, but there was never the shattering into small pieces that the old-fashioned conventional revolutionist dreamed of.[21]

Lawyers specialized in these sales, and some of them made a very good thing of it.

William Paterson, a member of the New Jersey Council of Safety, attorney-general of that state, later the leader of the small-state bloc in the constitutional convention of 1787, later still a Supreme Court justice, got rich dealing in confiscated estates.[22]

After he had fled to England, Joseph Galloway's big

handsome town house on the southeast corner of Sixth and Market streets in Philadelphia was appropriated by the state for the president of the Supreme Executive Council, but it eventually wound up in the hands of that canny speculator Robert Morris, sometimes called the Financier of the Revolution. Galloway's country place in Bucks County was to fall to the notorious General James Wilkinson.[23]

Confiscation was not a federal action. It was done by states; and the states, as the war wore on, grew increasingly aware of its value as a backer of currency, for they too, like the Continental Congress, were issuing worthless paper money right and left. As late as January 1782, after the shooting war had ceased, Georgia was using a new batch of confiscated Tory estates as security for the emission of £22,100 in shinplasters. That same state of Georgia was to give the Rhode Island blacksmith-turned-soldier Nathanael Greene the extensive properties seized from the Loyalist Lieutenant Governor John Graham, as a reward for his services as commander of the Army of the South. It was on this estate, some years later, that a house guest of the general's widow, a young Yankee named Whitney, was to invent the cotton gin.

The last large grant of grabbed land, however, was to be handed out by the Tories themselves; and this was the aftermath of what is generally regarded as the last military action of the war. The gallant Colonel Andrew Deveaux, a smashing, slashing Loyalist, having found no room left in which to fight in his native South Carolina, which by that time had been given over entirely to the Patriots, in April of 1783 took a force of two hundred Loyalist volunteers—known, for reasons that have not survived, as the Royal Foresters—from St. Augustine, Florida, to New Providence, the capital of the Bahama Islands. The Bahamas had recently been taken, or retaken, by Spanish forces from New Orleans under the redoubtable Galvez, for Spain, an ally of France, was still at war with Great Britain. Deveaux, in an action that was brilliant but bloodless, seized New Providence for the Crown, and with it the entire group of islands. For this he and his men were rewarded by a grant of six thousand acres on one of the islands, Eleuthera.

The carrot-and-stick peace approach of the Howe brothers having proved a failure, the British government tried once more to deliver too little too late. In April of 1778 the Duke of Richmond in the House of Lords moved for the recognition of independence of the American colonies—and was hooted down. At that same time there was making up the final peace-offering commission, which was authorized to concede practically everything *but* independence. This was headed by Frederick Howard, fifth earl of Carlisle, a bad-tempered young nobleman—he was still in his twenties—who seemed to think that he would be doing America a great favor by visiting it in person.

Many fanfares saluted the crossing of this commission; but when the would-be peace-makers reached Philadelphia they learned that General Clinton was about to evacuate it, going back to New York. Nobody in Whitehall had thought to tell the commissioners about this, though Clinton had had his orders for several weeks before the commission sailed from England. The Continental Congress—"Congo" the Loyalists like to call it—would consent to talk only on two preconditions: that all British troops be withdrawn from America and that independence be acknowledged. Baffled, the commissioners fell back upon their English political training and tried to offer certain selected congressmen bribes. They were laughed at.

Precisely as the British army leaders could not bring themselves to believe that such unsoldierly-seeming natives would fight, so the politicians, civilians, always were puzzled

and confused by the refusal of the Americans to leap at the
lure of bribery. It seemed unnatural. It seemed perverse.

The Loyalists in Philadelphia, who had come out fully
for the British side during that long merry winter in the city,
now were verging on panic. What would happen to them?
The Carlisle commissioners did pass out specific sums of
money to Loyalists who came to them with tales of woe, but
even with a big treasure chest they could not handle them
all, and the grumbling was loud.

From a London newspaper:

> In seventeen hundred-and-seventy-seven
> General Burgoyne set out for Heaven;
> But, as the Yankees would rebel,
> He missed the route, and went—to Hell.

And again:

Burgoyne, alas, unknowing future fates,
Could force his way through woods, but not through Gates.

All the clack had it that as a result of Burgoyne's surrender at Saratoga the French were about to enter the war,
and Carlisle, the old Etonian, seemingly was trying to forestall such an action when he blasted the French in his public
proclamations. The Marquis de Lafayette, who was even
younger than Carlisle, challenged him to a duel. Carlisle
coldly replied that as a royal commissioner he was responsible for his words only to his own government, which made
the Frenchman look rather foolish. All other appearances of
foolishness, however, were on the British side. The proclamations promised amnesty to Patriots who would sign an at-
testation of loyalty to the Crown; it fell flat, and amid a
deafening silence the commissioners crept home.

This could be said to mark a turning-point in the war, as far as the Loyalists were concerned. The men at Whitehall were beginning to understand that while America might still be filled with warmhearted subjects who were being persecuted by a fanatical and irresponsible minority, and who asked only to be released from bondage and to be restored to their proper places of worship, it might be necessary in order to get at these people to use different military methods. It might indeed even be necessary to do something about those people themselves.

There were many plans. In 1779 somebody proposed to establish an all-time Neutral Ground, a permanent settlement for the non-belligerent Loyalists, in the disputed colony of Vermont. Lord Germain favored a similar plan, carving out a new colony, a fully Tory colony, between the Penobscot and St. Croix rivers in Canada and northern Maine, the Royal Navy to protect this place, where each attested Loyalist would be given as much land as he had lost to the rebels, up to one thousand acres, all this to be free of quitrents for ten years. Elaborate maps were drawn, elaborate plans made; but nobody went to Maine. Then there was Colonel James Chalmers, a prominent Maryland Loyalist, who proposed, 15 September 1778, that land between the Delaware River and Chesapeake Bay be so used. Nothing came of this.

On the other hand, the home office thought, perhaps it might be best to enlist these true subjects, so that they might fight, as so long they had asked? They had displayed not the slightest interest in settling any of the proposed enclaves of Loyalism; they did not fancy the prospect of being roped off like lepers; so perhaps they would be willing to serve in the field?

Until this time the official British attitude had been that American Loyalists should only be used as escort troops, militiamen who could stand guard duty, or laborers. The thought of treating them as real soldiers, like the lobsterbacks, never had come into the English military mind. It came now.

New York City still was held, and firmly held, but the plan to split the colonies down the middle by taking over the whole length of the Hudson River had collapsed with Burgoyne's surrender. Whitehall now was inclined to believe with General Clinton that the place to fight the war was in the South, which could be taken over piecemeal. Without the South to supply them with food, the middle and New England colonies, cut off from the rest of the world by the navy as they were, could be starved into submission. Besides it was fondly believed that the southern colonies were crammed with staunch supporters of the Crown who only waited for the chance to spring to arms and put the horrid rebels down.

So—the war was moved to the South.[24]

The Patriots at this same time also decided that they should do something about the Loyalists in their midst. Those who had taken refuge in Canada or in New York were out of reach, of course, but there were many who stayed at home, keeping their fingers crossed. The trouble was, how could they be identified? how could you tell a dastardly Tory from a merely quiet true believer? One wag proposed that all Tories' houses should be painted black, but this suggestion was brushed aside. Instead, a series of tests was applied.

These tests differed from state to state, and differed from one another inside of the same state, as local conditions, local prejudices, had much to do with their application; but the person most interested in their strict enforcement was rather more than likely to be a real estate speculator.

Some Tories were merely declared, in print, to be "incorrigible." Others, as in North Carolina, were adjudged to be "objects of the resentment of the public" or else "under suspicion of being inimical to America," which meant that they were fair prey for anybody who had an ax to grind—or a fortune to make.

A respected authority [25] classes the laws against Loyalists as "harsh" in Massachusetts, New Jersey, and Pennsylvania; "harshest" in New York and South Carolina; "light" in Rhode Island, Connecticut, Virginia, and North Carolina; and "lightest" in New Hampshire, Delaware, Maryland, and Georgia. They were to stay on the books for a long while after the fighting was finished.

7

Big Man in Bavaria

THERE IS NO ACCOUNTING for Benjamin Thompson. There is something that doesn't come to us down over the years, that does not appear in the four fat volumes of essays and scientific treatises he published, or show in the various portraits of him by Gainsborough and others.

No stars danced at his birth, so far as we know. The event took place in Woburn, Massachusetts, 26 March 1753. His forebears on both sides had lived in those parts for more than a hundred years, being originally from England; so it was a fact that this outstanding European had no European background. There were no geniuses among those ancestors, no freaks—none, even, who showed promise. Benjamin himself was the freak of the family. He had several brothers and a sister, but we know nothing about them. He was orphaned early, in his lower teens, and after graduation from the local grammar school, his only formal education, he got a job as clerk in a dry goods store in Boston. He was a mathematical wizard who loved to tinker with scientific instruments, noting the results on paper, and once he almost blew his own face off when a chemical test misfired. He

71

attended a series of lectures at Harvard, though he was
never enrolled as a student there. Soon he was teaching
school himself, and it was as a teacher that he got a job in
Rumford, New Hampshire.[26] What he taught is not clear;
but he taught *himself* both French and German, and also he
learned to play the violin.

It was at Rumford that he did the first thing that
marked him as a man on the make. It was an accepted
English practice, though one not often resorted to in America. He married money.

He was nineteen years old, she thirty-three. She was
the widow of a militia colonel, the daughter of the town's
late beloved pastor. She owned a large farm.

All unabashed, Thompson began to operate this place.
Two deserters from a British regiment stationed at Boston
applied to him for jobs, and he took them on. There was
nothing unusual about this. Desertion was common at
Boston, despite the terrible punishments, and the deserters
customarily put a long distance between themselves and
their barracks before they looked around for work. They
were less likely to become farmhands, despite the lack of
seasonal labor in those parts, than drill sergeants; for their
knowledge of professional soldiery, of "the discipline"—the
manual-of-arms we would call it today—caused them to be
highly valued by backcountry militia officers. The two who
toiled for the Thompsons soon came to the conclusion that
such work was not for the likes of them, and they would
have gone back to their regiments, they told young Benjamin, if they could be sure that they would not be flogged.
Floggings, a routine army punishment, were particularly
severe at this time. Men died under them, or were perma-
nently crippled, or came out of the ordeal gibbering idiots.
Mr. Thompson, sir, knew the general at Boston; and could
he maybe write to him and get an agreement that such

savagery would be waived if the farmhands turned themselves in? Mr. Thompson said that he would do so, gladly.

He had met General Gage, commander-in-chief of all of His Majesty's military forces in America, at Boston, when he visited that city with his wife. Gage, an amiable man, married to an American, a New Jersey girl, was most anxious to keep the Americans quiet and happy—at least until he could retire at full pay, very soon. Benjamin Thompson could scarcely have become intimate with the general, who was also at this time Governor of Massachusetts, but he did not hesitate to write in behalf of the discontented farmhands. Whether or not his letter won them forgiveness is not a matter of record and doesn't matter anyway. What *does* matter was that Benjamin Thompson had corresponded, however briefly, with the enemy.

Some kind of war was coming closer all the time. Patriots in the hinterland as in the capital were tightening their ranks. Newcomers were scrutinized with even more than the usual suspicion, and this was especially true in the militia, which was, in effect though not in name, a political body, serving much the same purpose as the city volunteer fire departments were to serve a little later. The officers of the New Hampshire militia did not like Benjamin Thompson being a major in their midst.

This appointment had caused a stir. Again, it was a result of Mrs. Thompson's connections. She had introduced her husband to her cousin Governor John Wentworth, who, impressed by him, named him to succeed to a majority that had just fallen open. The Wentworths virtually owned New Hampshire, and with some reason considered the governorship a family fief; and it may be that Governor John supposed that nothing could weaken his position. But the militia officers were miffed. In God's name, who was this tall, admittedly good-looking lad who had never shouldered a musket, never tramped a parade ground, who was he to be hailed as a major and saluted? The townfolk had him brought before an unofficial meeting to face a charge of "being unfriendly to the cause of liberty." He was acquitted of this, but the hard feeling persisted, and he had reason to believe that a tar-and-feathers party would call on him some night. So he cleared out. He went back to Woburn, where he puttered about with further scientific experiments, and where his wife and their baby daughter joined him for a little while. All the talk was of war. The situation was tense.

Thompson was a friend of Dr. Benjamin Church, and he *might* have been the mysterious intruder who ransacked Church's desk, removing many papers, before the men who had arrested Church on a charge of treasonous correspondence could get there. This has been suggested by several historians, and it certainly was a physical possibility; but there is no proof that such a thing happened.

Thompson said, later, that he had offered his services to the forming Continental Army, but these services were refused. There is no record of this. Anyway, Mrs. Thompson and the baby went back to Rumford, while Benjamin went to Boston. Here was an open avowal, his first. Now he was an out-and-out Loyalist.

He was never to see his wife again. She died soon afterward.

The *wunderkind* did not walk or ride into Boston by land, over the Neck, for the city since Lexington-Concord had been in a state of siege, and such a passage would have been difficult, even dangerous. Instead he went to Rhode Island, where he took a ship. This was a common Loyalist procedure at the time.

Once among friends, he made no concealment of his sentiments, but offered himself and all of his military experience to the Loyalist movement.

Timothy Ruggles, a French and Indian War veteran, a brigadier in the Massachusetts militia, had attended the Stamp Act Congress as a delegate, but had refused to subscribe to its recommendations. Now that war had erupted he picked his side, unhesitatingly, reporting to General Howe (Gage had been recalled) and being put in charge of an effort to raise a Loyalist Legion in Boston, which was crammed with refugees. Ruggles accepted young Thompson as his second-in-command, or at least *one* of the seconds, and there was a great deal of drum-beating and flag-flapping, but nothing came of this movement. The truth is, the siege of Boston was just about finished. The city, practically an island, was doing the British no good, for, as Lexington-Concord had taught them, they could not venture out of it without being stung, and strategically anyway it meant little. Howe some time since since had decided that New York was the city he wanted. New York, and control of the north-south Hudson River, would cut the colonies in half, block off New England from the rest, and stifle the revolt. Even before George Washington had fortified Dorchester Heights with cannons brought all the way from Ticonderoga by the unquenchable Henry Knox, Howe had started making arrangements for a pullout to Halifax, where he would be heavily reinforced and from where he could descend unpent upon New York. He spiked such guns as he could not carry with him, burned such supplies as he could not immediately use, arranged somehow for transportation to Nova Scotia of about eleven hundred Loyalists, and on 17 March 1776 quitted Boston. (The day was to be celebrated every year for many years, but as Evacuation Day, not because it happened to be St. Patrick's Day, for this was well before the Irish invasion of the Hub City.) Major Thompson was told off to carry the news of this event, officially, to the British government. It was the sort of assignment that a later generation would describe as cushy, the sort of assignment the smart young officers at headquarters were always scheming to get.

The man in charge of the war in America, the man called upon to put down the revolt, was the secretary of state for colonies, Lord George Germain. He was lean, arrogant, astringent, and so brimming with blue blood that he found it hard even to communicate with ordinary, lowborn personages. As Lord George Sackville—he had taken the name of Germain as part of a new inheritance, though already a very rich man—he had been in charge of the English cavalry at the battle of Minden, and in this capacity had refused to charge the enemy, though repeatedly commanded to do so by the general, Prince Ferdinand of Brunswick. His reasons may have ben personal: he couldn't abide the prince. Anyway, this extraordinary refusal caused what should have been a sweeping victory to end as a stalemate, and public indignation ran high. At his own insistence, the English cavalry chief faced a court-martial, which found him guilty. He was cashiered. His name was read out of the army, publicly, before each regiment. It was solemnly decided that he was "unfit to serve his Majesty in any military capacity whatever." So now this was the man designated to put down the revolution in America, a land three thousand miles away, about which he knew nothing.

He was not alone in his ignorance. After Lexington-Concord and after Bunker Hill, Englishmen at home were asking one another, in bewilderment, what *was* going on over there? Did those colonists really mean what they said? Military men who in the Seven Years War had mixed with the colonials—no more, of course, than had been absolutely necessary—repeatedly assured their fellow countrymen that the American colonist was a coward who wouldn't fight. By any chance could these chaps have been mistaken? At the time of the evacuation of Boston, in itself an upsetting event for the average Englishman, anybody on that side of the sea who knew anything at all about America was enjoined to tell it, and Benjamin Thompson, who knew everything, was regarded as a Godsend. They flocked around him, and graciously he consented to enlighten them. That was right, he said, Americans wouldn't fight; the American military potential was next to nil, and such forces as had been raised were ludicrous, a collection of clowns.

Lord Germain was narrow of mind, but no fool. He had vindicated himself of the charge of cowardice, having met his man in the field of honor and permitted two clear shots, which he coolly refused to return. He knew that he was in the cabinet only because, his family connections being what they were, it would have been almost impossible to keep him out. He was determined to straighten the mess that was the northern department of the secretaryship of state, including the American colonies, and he set about slashing red tape at a high rate of speed. But he needed advice, something he was too proud to take from those around him, those within reach. He needed information. His own generals, he knew, took orders from him only because they were obliged by regulations to do so; and not a one of them, with Minden in mind, would have spoken to him on the street or in a drawing room. Lord Germain was irascible; he was unbearable; he thought he was God. But— he welcomed Benjamin Thompson with open arms. He treated him like a human being.

Thompson, still in his twenties, became Germain's shadow, and he had the title, and the pay, of an under-secretary of state. He was given a regular army commission, a lieutenant colonelcy of dragoons: it was an honorary spot, and he was not expected to appear on the field.

Germain was not a sociable man, so it could not be said

of these two that they were seen everywhere together; but it *could* be said that they were seldom seen apart. They ate together, all meals, including breakfast. They worked together. There were even those in London who whispered that they probably slept together; but there was no basis for this slander.

Germain took him along almost every time he went to see the King, which in periods of crisis was daily. The King too liked him.

The North cabinet fell, as, after Yorktown, it was bound to do. Whether by coincidence or whether it had been planned, Colonel Thompson got out just before the crash. He went to the Continent,[27] announcing as he did so that he was about to offer his sword to the Empire, helping to hold back the Turks. He never got as far as Vienna, and the sword remained unbloodied. In Paris quite by chance he encountered Prince Maximilian of Zweibrücken, nephew and heir apparent of the King of Bavaria. Max had just returned from America, where he headed one of the crack French regiments, that of Deux-Ponts. He was fascinated by Thompson and introduced him to the court of Bavaria, persuading his uncle to make him minister of war and then minister of police, at the same time.

Before he could accept these honors young Thompson must get the personal permission of the King, so he went back to England, where George III cheerfully obliged, knighting him into the bargain—*Sir* Benjamin.

Back in Catholic Bavaria the Protestant philosopher Thompson soon became chancellor. He reorganized the police department, as he reorganized the army, from top to bottom. He introduced sanitation, urging a scientific diet. He pioneered the potato in southern Germany. He cleared the streets of beggars. He was made a major general, he who had never fired a gun or been fired upon. He was created a nobleman of the Holy Roman Empire. He chose Rumford for his place-title: the Count of Rumford.

All the time he was carrying on experiments and writing papers for scientific societies. He belonged to more such societies than he could count. He is credited with being the first to state that heat is motion.

On a visit to England—he always protested that he loved England the best—he met an American visitor, his own daughter Sarah, whom he had not seen since her babyhood twenty-odd years before. He took her to Munich and introduced her in court. He got a pension for her, and the honorary title of Countess. She found him amusing, he was so serious about everything, but she refused to stay in Bavaria with him, returning, instead, to Concord, Massachusetts, where, never marrying, she lived to be a very old woman, demanding, always, that she be addressed as Countess.

It was a custom of the time for Central European grand dukes and princelings to uphold the validity of monarchism by authorizing outside administrators to initiate sweeping reforms, thus proving that they were enlightened. When he succeeded to the throne of Bavaria, Maximilian found Count Rumford, as his uncle had, the answer to a sovereign's dream. The former Benjamin Thompson for fourteen years virtually *was* the government of Bavaria: you can see his statue in Munich today.

When he retired, full of honors and still writing papers on the expansion of heat, it was to Paris, when in October of 1805 he married the widow of Antoine Laurent Lavoisier, the chemist who had been beheaded in the French Revolution. She was a woman of independent means—and independent ideas. She took the name of her new husband, but insisted upon retaining that of the first husband as well, being known thereafter as Madame Lavoisier de Rumford.

The marriage was a resounding failure. The fought in public, and no doubt in private as well. They locked each other out. They insulted each other's friends. At last they broke up, though the lady was to be called Madame Lavoisier de Rumford for the rest of her life.

President John Adams in 1799 offered Count Rumford a commission as inspector-general of artillery in the U.S. Army if he would undertake to lay out and to open the proposed new military academy at West Point. The count declined, regretfully, though he protested that he had always loved America. He did leave to the academy all of his books and original papers on the military art. The rest of his library he left to Harvard, where he endowed a chair of philosophy. He died, in Paris, 21 August 1814.

Historians of Loyalist leanings often cite Count Rumford as an example of the high type of man the independence movement drove out of America. But *was* he a Loyalist? Probably he himself didn't know. It is likely that he had no thoughts on the subject, and if he had any settled beliefs about independence he never did permit them to show. He has sometimes been compared with Benjamin Franklin, that convinced and knowledgeable Patriot. But this is ridiculous. Despite the multiplicity of his interests his mind was too much taken up with the advancement of Benjamin Thompson ever to be called broad; and he was not one-tenth the man that Franklin was.

8

An Abomination before the Lord

BY NO MEANS all of those who settled the first English colonies in America were looking for religious liberty. The Dutch, the Swedes, and Germans: these had made no complaint about ideological persecution at home; nor had the Scots, or the Irish; and many of the English settlers too had been content on this score, seeking, rather, *economic* legroom.

The men of the original Jamestown company—and they all were men—were as a matter of course members of the Church of England. It wouldn't have occurred to them to be anything else. The Bishop of London was a stockholder in the company that promoted this venture, which might account for the fact that this and subsequent American colonies were considered a part of the see of London. The bishops were not notably interested. None of them ever sent a suffragan across the sea; it is hard to see why. A few did send *commissaries*, men whose authority was never clearly defined, so that the local priests were leery of them, treating them at arm's length. The commissaries could not ordain. Any American who wished to become an Anglican priest must make the long, perilous, and expensive voyage across the sea to where a real bishop could lay his hands on him while uttering the proper words. Not many colonists were dedicated enough, or rich enough, to do that.

Early in the eighteenth century the Church of England became aware of the empire sufficiently to establish the Society for Propagating the Gospel in Foreign Parts, which was to set up many Episcopal churches in America and where necessary to help support them with private funds. It also made some pretense of carrying the Word of God to the Indians and even, a little, to the Negro slaves, though it never was to approach the missionary efforts of the Roman Catholic Church in French Canada, Latin America, and the West Indies: the Spaniards alone maintained seven archbishops and forty-one bishops in America.

The S.P.G.—that condescending name!—was not liked in America. The established priests saw their positions threatened by it, though they, at least, approved the stand the society took in favor of establishing a bishopric or two or even three in the colonies. This proposal horrified the members of all the non-Anglican denominations, and in particular the Congregationalists of New England, to whom lawn sleeves were an abomination before the Lord, in a class with incense, altar boys, confessionals, and all the rest of the Romish apparatus.

> Will they never let us rest in peace—except where all the weary are at rest? [cried the Boston preacher Jonathan Mayhew.] Is it not enough that they persecuted us out of the Old World? Will they pursue us into the New?—to convert us here, compassing sea and land to make us proselytes, while they neglect the heathen and heathenish plantations? What other New World remains as a sanctuary for us from their oppressions, in case of need? Where is the Columbus to explore one of us, and pilot us to it, before we are

consumed by the flames, or deluged in a flood of Episcopacy? [28]

There were many who felt that way. How, in any
event, could the colonies possibly afford a bishop, much less
bishops? Such a personage was a peer, a lord; and lords
were looked at askance in colonial America. A bishop lived
in a palace. He was attended perforce by a large retinue. A
thousand pounds a year would be required to keep such a
dignitary in the style to which he was supposed to be accustomed, and where were the colonies to find money like
that?

Even the colonial governors were opposed. Most of them,
appointed by the throne, were Church of England men,
and what with this fact and their little courts of hangers-on
and office-holders, also their state coaches, a great deal of
snobbism attached to the governorships—though that word
itself had not yet been concocted. Thomas Hutchinson had
been hailed in Massachusetts not only as a native son, no
import from England, but also as a staunch Congregationalist; and it was a large part of his fall from popularity that
he began to toy with Episcopalianism and soon became an
out-and-out convert.

The colonial legislatures controlled the purse strings. It
was they who appropriated the money for the gubernatorial
salary, which they set in the first place; and so they could
keep the governors in line. But the pomp of the office, if
somewhat sleazy, was pleasant; it was different, and flatter-
ing; and the presence of a bishop might well dim its glitter.

These were conditions in the Middle and New England
states, but in the South too, though the Church of England
had been formally established there, many, including most
of the Anglican priests themselves, were opposed to the idea
of an American bishop. The priests were an easy-living lot
down there, some of them little better than what today

would be called remittance men, and they looked with a jaundiced eye at the possibility of a bishop in their midst, a man who would enforce a most unwelcome discipline.

Nobody will ever know, for there is not a scale by which to measure it, but there can be little doubt that the Lawn Sleeves Controversy, the hottest issue in America at one time, had a great deal to do with bringing about the Revolution.

The tsarlike power of the first New England preachers had not passed entirely. It was not what it had been in the days of Hester Prynne and the embroidered "A" she had been forced to wear on her breast, but it still was a powerful force all up and down the seaboard, and inland as well, especially east of the Hudson, especially, that is, among the Congregationalists, who most fervently hated and feared the in-pushing Episcopalians.

The preacher often also was the teacher, and always he was the chief counsellor, the best-educated man in town or in that particular part of the countryside.[29] The preacher was a public figure, and as likely as not was followed in the streets.

Political oratory, though it was beginning to burst upon the common consciousness, had not yet become an accepted art. This was, rather, the age of the sermon, which was the discourse from which most men imbibed their beliefs. There was a sermon on every conceivable occasion, indoors or out, and it was esteemed the most important part of the program. Nobody would go anywhere or do anything of weight without first having listened to and brooded upon a sermon. It was a sermon that sent the muffled, shivering, lanthorned patriots up Bunker Hill on a certain memorable night, a sermon that was to move the backcountrymen east from Sycamore Shoals over the Blue Ridge to smite the Tories hip and thigh at King's Mountain, their battle slogan being "The sword of the Lord and of Gideon." Sermons were preached—and listened to—at weddings, town meetings, funerals, and the semi-annual drills and get-togethers of the village militia companies. If the pulpit no longer was all-powerful, at least it was a sounding-board that carried farther than the schoolmaster's desk, the judge's bench, or even the mansion of the governor.

The preacher, remember, was a natural leader, and assumed his responsibilities as such. He wasn't the fiery-eyed, semi-illiterate zealot of the frontier, who howled and swayed as he screeched, who chomped tobacco whilst misquoting the Good Book, for this was a figure not yet emergent on the American scene; but he was a *learned* man, quite possibly the only one for many miles around, who could, and often mercilessly did quote Luther, Calvin, Sydney, Pufendorf, Milton, Coke, Burnet, Butler, Tillotson, as well as Hobbes, Locke, Montesquieu, and even, sometimes, unexpectedly, Voltaire. The old-time New England man of God knew his Latin and Greek, and likely enough had more than a smattering of Hebrew as well; but most of all he knew his flock, his dependents, whom he must guide, by force if necessary.

It has been estimated [30] that at the time of the Revolution there were 3,105 churches in the English colonies of America. These were divided almost evenly among the New England provinces, the middle provinces, and the South, with about 1,000 for each. Of these the Congregationalists had 658, most of them in New England; the Presbyterians 543, mainly in the middle colonies; the Baptists 498, Anglicans 480, Quakers 295, German and Dutch Reformed 251, Lutherans 151.

There were few Catholics, and most of what there were were Patriots.

There were even fewer Jews, and virtually *all* of *them* were Patriots.

Of those who had come over on the *Mayflower* only

about half were seeking freedom of religion. They had called themselves the Saints or Pilgrims. They were not Puritans. The Puritans, who came later, aspired to purify the Church of England from within. The Pilgrims were Separatists, in law a sinful thing, or Brownists, as they sometimes called themselves, though the Reverend Robert Browne in fact some time since had made his peace with the Anglican church and was back in its good graces, preaching orthodoxy.

Theoretically at least, *ecclesiastically*, though this did not happen in New England, the Methodists of America were direct descendants of the Puritans, and at the time of the Revolution were still an integral part of the Church of England. They were split in their political views. John Wesley himself was a staunch Loyalist, but many, including Francis Asbury, the first Methodist bishop in America, were Patriots. They had thirty-seven churches, most of them in Maryland and Virginia.

It was often said that the Baptists, like the Congregationalists, were Patriots largely because the Episcopalians were Loyalists; and this could be true; for non-Episcopalians in colonial America tended to treat the Episcopalians with the same fear and suspicion that they had used toward the Roman Catholics, not as overblown, slightly pretentious, but essentially all-right companions in religion, but rather as fiends, persons inherently, violently evil.

The political position of the Episcopalians never was in doubt. They were, after all, members of a state church. Their ministers were required to pray for the King and the royal family, to whom these same men, when they were ordained, had taken an oath of allegiance. In Maryland, Virginia, and the Carolinas, the Church of England was an established church, the only officially recognized church, supported by taxes, as was done in England. Yet it was precisely in those colonies that the Episcopacy was the weakest. In part this was because of the taxation, which was resented; and in part it must have been because, candidates for the priesthood not being forthcoming in America, there were sent to the Carolinas and Virginia a succession of misfits, weaklings, drunkards whom the Church no longer wished to harbor at home. The Congregationalists were "established" in that sense, too, in Connecticut, New Hampshire, and Massachusetts, though the clergymen there were strong, outspoken men, and no such conditions prevailed.

The Church of England was to remind the world, afterward, that more than half of the fifty-six signers of the Declaration of Independence were Episcopalians. This is true, though there were no wearers of the cloth among them. The outbreak of the American Revolution posed a very real problem for the Episcopal ministers in America, most of whom were dependent upon their salaries. They met it in different ways.

There was Reverend John Beach of Newton, Connecticut, who carried on the same as before, despite threats of violence. He contended afterward that he was actually fired upon once while he was in the pulpit—though nobody else seems to have heard the shot.

There was Reverend Aeneas Ross, a brother-in-law of Betsy the flag-maker, who kept his Anglican church in Delaware open all through the war by the simple process of omitting the prayers for the royal family, which nobody seemed to miss. Other ministers were wont to substitute mumbled gibberish for the words of the Book of Common Prayer at this point, justifying themselves in their own consciences afterward by contending that *they* knew what those words *really* meant.

There was Dr. Charles Inglis, the assistant rector of Trinity Church, New York, who after holding out as long as he could, went to England—and became the first bishop of Nova Scotia.

There was the Reverend Samuel Seabury of New York, originally of Connecticut, who endured even more. Like Inglis, he was a Tory writer of great distinction and influence. He was the author of a best-seller, a Loyalist appeal, *Letters of a Westchester Farmer,* which goaded a young King's College student fresh up out of the West Indies, one Alexander Hamilton, into answering it. Harassed at home, Seabury fled to New York City, where he became chaplain of one of the Loyalist regiments for the remainder of the war. After the war he went to England, meaning to become a bishop. As an American citizen—which he was, in spite of everything—he could not take the oath of allegiance to King George, and therefore no English bishop would consecrate him. This was done by three Scottish bishops of the Anglican Church, who suffered no such limitations of power, and the Reverend Mr. Seabury returned to what was by that time a republic as the first bishop of the Protestant Episcopal Church of the United States.

There was the Reverend Jacob Duché, son of a former mayor of Philadelphia, a graduate of Cambridge University, an Anglican deacon, rector of the united parishes of Christ Church and St. Peter's in Philadelphia, and married to a sister of Francis Hopkinson, the poet-lawyer-flautist, who was best known as the man who designed the Stars and Stripes. The Reverend Mr. Duché was one of the most popular sermonizers in the capital, and the Second Congregational Congress chortled with delight when he consented to become its chaplain. He opened every session of the Congress with a prayer—until the time when, at the approach of the British, Congress scampered away to York, Pennsylvania. Later—he having resigned as Congressional chaplain in the meanwhile—the Reverend Mr. Duché, through a mu-

tual friend—a middle-aged, respectable, unsuspecting widow
—sent a letter to General Washington, 15 October 1777, in
which he urged the commander-in-chief to ask Congress to
rescind the Declaration of Independence or else to "negotiate for your country at the head of your Army." Washington was stunned, the blow was so unexpected, but he read
on:

> Can you have the least confidence in a set of un-
> disciplined men and officers, many of whom have been
> taken from the lowest of the people, without principle,
> without courage? Take away them that surround your
> own person, how very few are there you can ask to sit
> at your table? . . . Take an impartial view of the pres-
> ent Congress, and what can you expect from them?
> . . . These are not the men that America has chosen
> to represent her. Most of them were chosen by a little,
> low faction, and the few gentlemen that are among
> them now are well known to lie on the balance, and
> looking up to your hand alone to turn the beam. 'Tis
> you, sir, and you only that support the present Congress;
> of this you must be fully sensible.[31]

Washington hastily sent the letter to Congress, which
got the greatest jolt of its career. The dismay, the black
despair, produced by this letter—which the Reverend Mr.
Duché obviously had meant only for Washington's own eye
—was at least as great as that brought about by the earlier
defection of Dr. Benjamin Church, though Duché never was
high in Patriot circles as Church had been. It should have
been muffled, but somebody leaked it to the Tories, and it
appeared in Rivington's *Royal Gazette* in New York 29
November. Duché cleared out for England, where he got an
appointment as secretary and chaplain for the Orphanage

for Females in Lambeth, while at home most of his property
was confiscated. He did not like England, and as soon as
the war was over he began to write to friends, Washington
among them, asking if his return could be arranged. He was
by that time a Swedenborgian and had suffered a paralytic
stroke. He was permitted to return to Philadelphia, though
only under a pledge never again to take any part in politics.
He lived until 3 January 1798, a highly unhappy man.

There was the Reverend Jonathan Boucher of Maryland, a prodigious penman, a satirist of real talent, whose
outspoken Loyalism won him so many enemies that he was
to boast after the war that he had preached every Sunday
with a pair of loaded and cocked pistols on the Bible-stand
before him. It would not be seemly to accuse a man of God
of sensationalizing, though it does seem in this case as
though the shot-at story of Reverend John Beach had
tempted Reverend Jonathan Boucher to emulation, with
trimmings. In those days, before the invention of the safety
catch, a loaded and cocked pistol was a thing in the presence
of which no man in his right mind would so much as sneeze.
If the Reverend Mr. Boucher really did place these weapons
on a surface upon which it can be assumed that he was wont
to pound he must have had an extraordinarily courageous
congregation. Anyway, that was his story, and he stuck to it.
He did not preach long in America after things got hot, but
in 1775 fled to England, where he became Vicar of Epsom,
and where he died.

There was the Reverend Mather Byles, a well-born
Boston Congregationalist whose Loyalism likewise was outspoken. He was sixty-nine years old, but full of fireworks.
The powers-that-be, after the departure of General Howe,
were afraid of the Reverend Mr. Byles, and they put him
under house arrest to keep him quiet. The presence of an
armed guard amused the cleric, who called him "my observe-

a-Tory." Soon this man was removed, but then he was put back, only to be removed again. "I have been guarded, regarded, and disregarded," Mr. Byles wrote to a friend. The old man switched to the Episcopal Church after the war was over, but he never did recover his popularity.

There was the entire faculty of King's College (later Columbia), which was solidly loyal. This consisted of the Reverend Myles Cooper, president; the Reverend John Vardill, regius professor of divinity, and Dr. Samuel Clossy, professor of astronomy and natural philosophy.

There was John Peter Gabriel Muhlenberg, the son of a Lutheran missionary, who himself was minister of a predominantly German congregation at Woodstock in the Shenandoah Valley of Virginia, where one Sunday in 1776 he finished a sermon in a most unusual manner, delighting future artists. He had been using for his text a familiar quotation from Ecclesiastes, the "a time to" text: "A time to be born, and a time to die . . . a time to break down, and a time to build up; A time to love, and a time to hate . . ." He interrupted himself with his own words: "A time to pray, and a time to fight," whereupon he peeled off his clerical robe, revealing a colonel's uniform beneath it, a uniform complete with epaulettes and clanking sword. He marched to the door, which he threw open, ordering the drums to beat for recruits. In a little while he had raised more than three hundred soldiers, who became the 8th Virginia, better known as the German Regiment, and he marched them off to join the newly authorized Continental Army.

The thing of course had been planned, and it came as no surprise to the worshippers. Moreover, John Peter Gabriel Muhlenberg was a Church of Englander in name only. He had studied theology under his own father, and had preached in sundry churches in New Jersey, when he was offered the pastorate of the Woodstock church, a large one.

He then learned that he could not practice any of the privileges of a clergyman in Virginia, where the Church of England was established—that is, he could not conduct weddings, funerals, and the like, which made up the greater part of a minister's income in Virginia in the eighteenth century—unless and until he had been ordained an Anglican priest. There still being no bishop in America, young Peter went to England, where he studied for another year, and where, 23 April 1772, the Bishop of London himself laid hands upon him, ordaining him. He never had been ordained a Lutheran minister, though he considered himself one.

Muhlenberg and his German volunteers served throughout the Revolution, at the Brandywine, at Germantown, and Stony Point; they endured the long terrible winters at Morristown and Valley Forge; they were present at the surrender at Yorktown. Muhlenberg had early been made a brigadier, and at the end of the war he became a major general. He was by no means the only clergyman who fought in the Continental Army, though he was the highest in rank, none other becoming more than a major. These were in addition to the chaplains, who came and went, whose status, semi-civilian, was ill-defined. "The Parson-General" they called him affectionately. He did not go back to his pulpit after the war, but went into politics instead, being elected to Congress.

9

All the Good Americans

THERE WERE about 2,600,000 persons in the British colonies of North America, and at the time when muskets began to bang along Concord road there were thirty-seven newspapers, most of them weeklies or semi-weeklies. Of these it has been estimated [32] that seven or eight were Loyalist, twenty-three were Whig, while the others had so far managed to evade the issue. There were nine colleges.

James Rivington was a long-nosed, high-strung young man in London, born to a publishing family and gaily following the family business. He made a lot of money publishing Smollett's *History of England,* and it went to his head. He lived high for a while and lost large sums at the racetrack at Newmarket, until at last bankruptcy stared him in the face. He pulled out in time, and succeeded in getting everybody paid off, but this left him so short of money that he decided he'd better go to America, the Happy Hunting Ground of English bankrupts. At thirty-six, then, he crossed the Atlantic. He opened a stationery shop in Philadelphia, then another in King Street, Boston, and still another in New York. He sold books as well, and did job printing. All three places were profitable, but the nervous Mr. Rivington was in a hurry—too much of a hurry—and he got mixed up

James Rivington receiving a visit from an enraged patriot, Ethan Allen

in a dark scheme known as the Maryland Lottery, only to become bankrupt once more.

He sold the Boston and the Philadelphia shops, and concentrated on New York. There, from his place in Hanover Square, 18 March 1773, he published a preliminary free issue of the *New-York Gazetteer; or, the Connecticut, New Jersey, Hudson's River, and Quebec Weekly Advertiser*. It was the first daily newspaper in America, and was a success from the start, running up a circulation of thirty-six hundred, a record.

Rivington used local news, but he made a special effort to get European news as well, questioning ships' skippers and their passengers, mixing with British officers and with traders at coffeehouses and in ordinaries, which suited his natural bent, for he was a convivial man. He borrowed letters and published them. He ran the best journal in the New World.

But the war clouds were gathering, and neutrality was no longer to be allowed, certainly not in a newspaperman. Rivington did try to give both sides, but his inclination was toward the conventional,[33] and this began to show in his editorials, so that the Sons of Liberty snarled. Like any editor he was used to threats, and he paid no attention to these.

He had recently moved his shop from Hanover Square to the foot of Wall Street, and it was there, 27 November 1775, that he was visited by Isaac ("King") Sears of Connecticut at the head of seventy-odd mounted Sons of Liberty. Rivington himself was lucky enough to be out at the time of his visit, and so he was not injured, but the Sons left very little of the printshop machinery, and none of the type at all. They declared before leaving that they would melt the type down for bullets, though whether this was ever done is not known. Metal was in short supply in the colonies. James Rivington again was destitute. He went back to England.

He returned two years later with a fresh font of type, new machinery, and a new title: he had been appointed King's Printer in America, and the *Royal Gazette*, which he proceeded to establish, was to be regarded as an official publication. The job carried a salary of £100 a year, but Rivington never did get any of that, for the terms of his appointment provided that the money was to come from New York quitrents, and there were no longer any quitrents in New York.

Since Rivington sailed away the British had taken over the city—first Staten Island, then Long Island, at last Manhattan itself—and they were to remain there for the rest of the war and even a little after that. The Patriots, however, still controlled the hinterland, which is where the quitrents would have come from, if there had been any.

Nevertheless, James Rivington, who was resiliency personified, did very well for himself.

"Propaganda" was still only an ecclesiastical word at that time; it was a Roman Catholic institution, not a false-slanting of information, of news; but this did not mean that such false-slanting did not occur. Newspapers printed the truth only when the truth was pertinent to their purposes. It was a side-line to them, an occasional spice, never an aim in itself. The reader *assumed* that it was up to him to decipher the ultimate story, to bare the fact, to dig out the nugget of truth, if there was one, and if he could do so. It was considered something of a game. *Caveat legens.*

Rivington was superbly well qualified for the task that he had to perform, but he could never hope to overtake the greatest news-twister of them all, a Patriot, Samuel Adams no less.

Adams for a long time had been writing under a variety of noms de plume for most of the Boston newspapers but chiefly for the *Boston Gazette*. This, the most influential periodical in town, was known by the Boston Tories as "the weekly dung barge." Adams didn't mind. He worked on in silence, a boll weevil of a man, hidden away, indefatigable.

The Hub City, before the outbreak of hostilities, was inundated with redcoats. These were an nuisance sometimes, but never a real menace. They were under strict orders not to molest the townspeople, who, in their eagerness to protect their own rights, were all too ready to cast the first stone. It must not seem so to the outside world, to the other colonies. There the citizens must be told that Boston was enduring an agony. Otherwise the fear might grow that Boston Whigs were perhaps going too far too fast.

Private letters were not enough. The aid of a press association was needed.

So Samuel Adams, at forty-seven, invented the news agency. He had some help from William Cooper and the printer Benjamin Edes, perhaps from a few others as well, but the idea was his, and so were most of the "reports." He did not slow his long-standing flow of letters to the local press. He simply wrote more, and he sent it forth.

The *Journal of Occurrences*, or *Journal of Events*, or *Journal of Happenings*, as it was variously called, was just a little extra work to be done late at night in the small untidy study in Purchase Street while his wife and children slept.

It was of course anonymous. It was in the form of a diary written by an always unnamed resident of Boston, and it went out every week by the regular post riders, free to the *New London Gazette*, the *New York Journal*, the *Pennsylvania Journal*, the *Maryland Gazette*, the *South Carolina Gazette*, and just about anybody else who wanted it. All of these were Whig publications, but many others would be sure to copy the "diary" from them, as was the custom.

It was operated for almost a year, never missing a week, from 28 September 1768 to 1 August 1769. It was a thumping success.

Some attempt was made in almost every number to report on the civic affairs of Boston, but by far the greatest part of the sheet was covered with accounts of atrocities committed by the visiting infantrymen.

Adams's friends were to contend that all of his stories, or most of them anyway, were founded upon real happenings. If this was so, then the principals involved never would have recognized themselves.

Did a lobsterback, stubbing his toe, curse the pain under his breath? This became a tirade, full of blasphemy and vituperation, directed at unresisting civilians.

Did one such slip in a puddle and inadvertently bump a passerby? This became a bloody and unprovoked attack.

Samuel Adams was a deeply religious man, an old-line Puritan, and he did not like to write about such things as sexual assaults. But he knew the call of duty when he heard it, and, wincing, he obeyed. According to the *Journal* outrages were happening every day all over town, where no woman was safe. Adams even bore down upon this phase of the occupation, sparing no details.

Most of the redcoats quartered in Boston could not read, but when accounts of these heinous doings were read to them invariably they expressed popeyed amazement. Why in bloody hell, they were wont to ask, would anybody take the trouble to rape a woman in Boston, where there were so many of them to be had for next to nothing? Nevertheless, the *Journal of Occurrences* came out week after week, waxing more horrific with each issue.

James Rivington could not hope to cope with such lying as this; but he did not need to try, for the situation had changed since he sailed from New York. The real war, a hot war, had broken out. The Continental Army had been organized, more or less. Gage had been recalled. Washington had fortified Dorchester Heights, forcing the British out. Howe had withdrawn to Nova Scotia, there to await enormous reinforcements, and then he had descended in crushing force upon New York.

Thereafter, it is true, William Howe did not do much. He had a well-trained and -equipped army, besides his Hessian mercenaries. He had the full use of a good part of the Royal Navy under the admiralship of his own brother, Lord Richard ("Black Dick") Howe. He had the time and the money with which to whip the badly demoralized Continentals; but he didn't seem to have the inclination. Perhaps he was confident that the Continentals, faced with such terrible odds, would sue for peace, something the Howe brothers in their capacity of royal commissioners had the authority to arrange. It might have seemed unthinkable to him that Washington would go on fighting, that his men would go on following him. Or perhaps Howe was just lazy. He had always been a man to take things easy. He gambled a great deal, as did his doxy, a dazzling blonde from Boston, Mrs. Joshua Loring, the former Elizabeth Lloyd, whom he took everywhere.[34] Also, he had just been knighted.

This month was remarkable for the investiture of General Howe with the order of the Bath; a reward for *evacuating* Boston, for *lying indolent* upon Staten Island for near two months, for *suffering* the whole rebel army to escape him upon Long Island, and *again* at the White Plains; for *not putting an end to rebellion* in 1776, when so often in his power; for making such *injudicious cantonments* of his troops in Jersey as he did, and for *suffering* 10,000 veterans under experienced generals, to be cooped up in [New] Brunswick, and [Perth] Amboy, for nearly six months, by about 6,000 militia, under the command of an inexperienced general.

So wrote crusty old Thomas Jones, a Yale man, class of '50, a New York provincial Supreme Court justice, and a rock-ribbed Loyalist.[35] Many felt as Judge Jones did. Even today there are those who believe that the Americans would do well to raise fewer statues to that uncertain shrieker William Pitt and more to General Howe, the great do-nothing man, the nation's best friend, a real Founding Father.

Rivington, then, on his return found himself at the very seat and headquarters of Loyalism in America—namely, New York. They came to that city from all directions, not just from upstate but from New Jersey and Pennsylvania as well, and from Connecticut. Each of them had his tale of woe; and each of them held his hand out, palm up.

They formed clubs. They drank coffee, also claret. They waited upon the general, complaining. They cooled their heels in anterooms. And naturally, since they sought for something to do, and since it so vigorously expressed their own political views, they read James Rivington's *Royal Gazette*.

He had, in effect, a captive audience. *Something* had to be done about these refugees, many of whom had been men of means whose property had been seized by the Patriots.

Like everybody else in the city they believed that the
crushing of the rebellion would be no more than a matter
of days, and meanwhile, of course, they should not be called
upon to do manual labor, as on one or two occasions was
suggested, bringing sniggers from the Patriots outside:

> Come, gentlemen Tories, firm, loyal and true,
> Here are axes and shovels and something to do!
> For the sake of your king
> Come labor and sing.

It was estimated that before the end of the war this
little colony of drones, all *Gazette* readers as a matter of
course, was costing the British government £40,280 a year,
besides all the "made" jobs.[36]

"But, alas, they all prate & profess much; but, when
you call upon them, they will *do* nothing," cried Howe's
private secretary to his diary.[37]

This is not true. Once the British had come to realize
that they had a real war on their hands, and that Washington, "the old fox," and his contemptible little army were not
going to fall into their laps like fruit from a fruit tree, once
they had called for regular army recruits from among the
refugees crowded into the city, agreeing to treat them like
men rather than like boresome poor relations, the response
was good. About fifty thousand Americans were to enlist as
regulars or militiamen, to fight and often to die for the
British; and of these at least fifteen thousand were from New
York, the heaviest contributor among the colonies.

Not to these enlistees but to the older, steadier refugees
—those who had come to New York for a few days or at
most a few weeks, waiting for the revolt to be put down,
but who found themselves perforce lingering in the uncomfortable city, where they were in effect prisoners—did

James Rivington pitch his *Royal Gazette*. He had mounted
the royal arms on his masthead now, complete with supporters, the lion and the unicorn fighting for the crown,
and he no longer made any pretense of impartiality. He
was an out-and-out Loyalist. He told them what they wanted
to hear, and his voice was shrill, his accents harsh.

General Robertson at the Parliamentary inquiry into
the war conduct of the Howe brothers, in 1779, testified
that a majority of Americans, "more than two thirds,"
wanted peace; and he defined the aim of the war as the
liberation of Americans, meaning, it must be assumed, the
liberation of that great majority who were held subjects
by those wild-eyed fanatics, the rebels.

"I never had an idea of subduing the Americans," he
said. "I meant to assist the good Americans subdue the bad."

This was understandable to the Tory exiles of London
and New York, the two biggest colonies of them. All of
these men were "good Americans," as the general saw it;
and they were unhappy. In London, some few still struggled
to make over the world, framing, as Joseph Galloway did,
papers that they hoped would somehow reach the king—
"The Case and Claim of the American Loyalists, impartially
stated and considered" and "The Claim of the American
Loyalists reviewed and maintained upon incontrovertible
Principles of Law and Justice," and many, many more—but
for the most part they could only foregather daily in some
favorite drinking place, the Jerusalem Tavern or the St.
Clemens' Coffee-House, or at the Adelphi in the Strand,
which was the headquarters of the New England Club, or
at the New-England Coffee House in Threadneedle Street,
or the Crown and Anchor in the Strand, and tell one another,
again, their mournful it-might-have-been tales.

In New York, a not dissimilar colony, they also tended

to meet according to places of origin; thus, the exiled Tories from Pennsylvania favored Birket's Tavern near Maiden Lane, while those from New Jersey went to Leonard's, those from Massachusetts to Hicks', and the Virginians patronized the Queen's Head.

These men did at least have the satisfaction of knowing that they were near home, so that when the truth prevailed, when the war ended, which of course would be any day now, they could the sooner resume the decent, reasonable, *loyal* lives that they had always been used to leading. They also had Rivington's *Royal Gazette*.

There was little enough military activity in those dreary crowded years in New York, but whatever there was Rivington proclaimed by means of a journalistic bass drum. Every skirmish in the outskirts was a brilliant victory for the King's forces. Every petty raid into New Jersey, every house-burning, was hailed as the Beginning of the End. The rebels were falling apart, their so-called leaders squabbling among themselves, while mutiny raged in the ranks. Several times the enterprising Mr. Rivington killed George Washington, and once he even killed Benjamin Franklin. It sold papers. (However, he never did go as far as the *London Morning Post*, which once carried a story to the effect that Martha Washington had left the general.)

Rivington's work was appreciated. He prospered. At one time he owned a half interest in a coffeehouse, though whether he had acquired this as an investment or as a news source is not clear. His first wife had died in England, and now in New York he remarried, successfully. He dressed in the height of fashion and lived well. He was pointed out.

When the war at last did end, the wrong way for the Loyalists, it must have seemed to those in New York like the end of the world. What couldn't have happened, had.

The British evacuate New York, 1783.

And the redcoats and the Hessians prepared to depart, and the poor relations began to wonder what it would be like in Nova Scotia. They were stunned, unbelieving.

The new governor, who would supervise the great withdrawal from the city, was Sir Guy Carleton. He appeared to like James Rivington; at least he arranged to get inactive army commissions at half pay for Rivington's two small sons.

The *Royal Gazette* folded early in 1783, though for some time Rivington was to keep up the job-printing business. Soon afterward the Patriots poured back in. The publisher, sometimes described as the most hated man in America, had prepared against this. He was not hanged and not even threatened with a tar-and-feathering; and this was because he had made his peace with General Washington, for whom he had been spying for some time.[38] But he no longer prospered, and no longer caused a stir when he walked the street. He died broke.

10

So Grotesque a Blunder

THE TROUBLE with Loyalism in the American Revolution was that it was a *negative* thing; it was not a burning belief, but rather an *absence* of belief; and there will always be trouble getting men to rally round a vacuity.

The Loyalists lacked leaders, which they did not seem to think they needed, and which the home country never even thought to supply.

For a long time the Loyalists did not see any need for developing or proclaiming an alternative to independence, and so they did nothing, smugly sure of themselves, certain that God was on their side. They did not even confer together or form Committees of Correspondence, as did the Patriots.[39] Sooner or later, they told themselves, the right would prevail. If worse came to worst, they told themselves further, the forces of the King would step in; and nobody could doubt what would happen then.[40]

That you can't beat something with nothing is an old American political adage, but it is not *that* old, and seemingly even the thought of it had not come to the pleased-with-themselves Tories, who clucked their tongues and shook sad heads as they watched the spread of the movement for independence. They had, in fact, nothing. They were in no condition to fight.

They had few newspapers, in most parts of the land no way at all in which to spread their ideas excepting by word of mouth—and with the Sons of Liberty scowling at them from behind every bush they had to guard their talk. Rather feebly, after a while, they began to assert that the Whigs—they refused to call them Patriots—so far from gaining independence were selling their souls to a pack of heartless, profane, unconscionable scoundrels. Congress was perfidious. The Whigs were called "sons of despotism"; but this didn't seem to do much good.

The strong characters among the American Loyalists had been driven into an early exile, like Thomas Hutchinson, or like William Franklin thrown into jail. Some of them were what were called, by both sides, "legality Tories," which meant that they were men who insisted that obedience to London was inherent in the law and that anything else was unthinkable; and though this was one way of looking at the problem, it was hardly inspiring and made no converts.

To be sure, the Loyalists had the King; but he was a man three thousand miles away, a fat man with eyes like ping-pong balls, a good family man, everybody said, but no commander; none of the pronouncements put forth in his name suggested that he was possessed of charm or perspicacity, much less common sense. The King was a dim abstraction, at first. He was soon to become an abomination.

When the first callers-out for liberty raised their voices in America they were careful not to decry the King. Everything, rather, was blamed upon the cabinet ministers, the assumption being that King George, God bless him, was in the hands of bad men who kept from him knowledge of the political conditions in his American colonies. It did not

seem to matter that no man worth his salt would have submitted to such "protection"; the King was the King. Thus,
the Redcoats stationed in Boston were known as the *ministerial* army, and sometimes too the warships were referred
to as the *ministerial* rather than the Royal Navy. It is easy
to smear politicians, who indeed often seem to exist for
that very purpose.

So there was kept up the myth that the King himself
was a kindly person much misled by those who surrounded
him, and seemingly both deaf and blind, poor fellow.

This was to change abruptly once the guns had begun
to go off. Americans learned that they could speak of George
III as an ignorant bigot and remain unstruck by thunder-
bolts; and they did so, with gusto. Perhaps Thomas Paine
had as much to do with this revelation as any person. An
Englishman himself, another bankrupt, only recently arrived
on western shores, he saw no reason to strew the customary
fulsome stuff about royalty across his pages when on 9
January 1776, in Philadelphia, he published *Common Sense.*
It was a smash hit, by far the biggest seller of its time, and
from it Americans learned to speak slightingly and to think
angrily about George III, "the royal brute of Britain." Paine
had no respect for the institution of monarchy, "the most
preposterous invention the devil ever set on foot for the
promotion of idolatry." As for divine right: "A French
bastard, landing with an armed banditti, and establishing
himself King of England against the consent of the natives,
is in plain terms a very paltry, rascally original. It certainly hath no divinity in it."

Americans gulped, but read on.

". . . the period of debate is closed. Arms, as a last
resource, must decide the contest . . . a hardened, sullen-
tempered Pharaoh . . . Of more worth is one honest man

to society, and in the sight of God, than all the crowned ruffians that ever lived." [41]

When a little later Thomas Jefferson sat down to write the Declaration of Independence, he too felt no need to pull verbal punches. Not "His Majesty" but "the King of England" was designated as a "tyrant." He was blamed for just about everything—the stirring-up of the Indians, the burning of the coastal towns, attempts at slave insurrections, the hiring of the Hessians and other German mercenaries,[42] the denial of the right of jury, the control of colonial judges, everything. After the celebrated preamble the whole paper was in effect an indictment of George III, every paragraph being an accusation: "He has refused . . . He has forbidden . . . He has dissolved . . . He has refused . . ." The longest and most strident paragraph even charged the King with conspiring to break up all colonial attempts to stamp out the slave trade, a subject very close to the heart of Thomas Jefferson, himself a slave owner. John Adams rubbered out his lips when he read "that vehement philippic," meaning the slave-trade paragraph, and he expressed doubt that a body like the Continental Congress, containing so many Southerners, would consent to pass upon it; but he himself made only trifling changes, changes in punctuation alone, as did the other committee member, Benjamin Franklin.

For four furiously hot days, the first four days of July 1776, the Congress discussed this document, pulling it apart, while Thomas Jefferson sat silent in a back seat, for he was a shy man and never one to speak in public if he could avoid it. Congress changed many things in modifying the original draft of the Declaration, on the whole softening it. The hot paragraph, the one about the slave traffic, it cut viciously, then lifted the whole thing out. At last it passed the resolution, and the word went forth, so that bells were rung and flags were run up and there were many cheers. In New York City a group of soldiers and civilians made their feelings clear when they threw ropes over an heroic equestrian statue of George III in the Bowling Green, and with one mighty tug toppled it to the pavement. The statue was gilded, but not gold. It was, in fact, made of lead. This was axed into handleable chunks and sent to a factory at Litchfield, Connecticut, where it was melted down and molded into bullets for the Continental Army: it made 42,088 bullets.

The Declaration in some cases cleared the air. After that to waver, to wobble, was inexcusable, all but impossible; and some grays slithered to the white side, but some slithered to the black. John Dickinson, though he had refused to sign the Declaration, remained in the Patriot camp, more or less. It was not so with Daniel Dulany, Maryland's most distinguished lawyer. Dulany had been born in America but educated in England, and it was he who, learnedly and definitely, had blasted to bits the complicated and rather shrill Tory argument that the American colonies were "virtually" represented in Parliament. The Declaration of Independence, however, was more than he could swallow, and he became an avowed Tory, albeit a very, very quiet one.

January 8, 1778, France did the long-expected when she announced that she was prepared to negotiate a mutual defense treaty with the new republic in America. France was the father and grandfather of war as the eighteenth century knew it. Just as all musical terms were Italian, so practically all military terms were French—redan, redoubt, flèche, regiment, demilune, gabion, saucisson, tenaille, chevaux-de-frise—attesting to the place of their birth. France had three times the population of Great Britain, ten times that of the American colonies. She had a bigger army than that of Britain and almost as large a navy.

The colonists had been scheming for this alliance for years; it had been their one hope for survival; and though they knew as well as anybody else that France was not offering to help out of the kindness of her heart, or in order to further the cause of democracy, but only because a union with the rebelling colonies offered such a wonderful chance to repay England for the humiliation of the peace imposed after the Seven Years War, still the alliance seemed a rope let down from heaven.

But—was it?

The Patriots greeted the news of the treaty with whoops of delight, the Continental soldiers with many a *feu de joie*, while everywhere bands played and crowds cheered. All the same, many an American must have wondered if this didn't mean a retaking of Canada by the French, which might make the colonial position worse than ever, and might cause the lost boss, Britain, to show in retrospect as a boon.

France was a traditional enemy. All the colonial wars had been against France and France's fierce Indian allies. There had been four of them, and though they were *officially* called by different names—King William's War, Queen Anne's War, King George's War, the Seven Years War—as far as the American colonists were concerned they were all, generically, the French and Indian War. France had not shown up well in these contests. France was untrustworthy. France was ambitious. Would she make a safe friend?

The Loyalists leapt upon this development with cries of glee. It might be supposed that an alliance between their enemy and the most powerful military nation on earth would seem, just at first anyway, a somewhat discouraging sign; but nothing could discourage the American Loyalists, who believed that the might of Great Britain was without any limit, and her cause just, and to whom even the surrender of Gentleman Johnny Burgoyne and his whole wilderness army seemed but a minor setback, to be brushed aside like a cobweb that has been walked into in the dark.

Now at last the Loyalists had something positive to shout. And shout they did! Their media were limited; for Boston and Philadelphia, after being held for only a little while, like Newport, had been evacuated, and Charleston had yet to be captured in the biggest British victory of the war, which left them only New York with its gaggle of pusillanimous periodicals, but there was nothing wrong with their lungs. *Now* for sure, they cried, the misled rebels were marching arm-in-arm into hell. *Now* they would be snapped up, chewed, swallowed.

> I'll tell these croakers how he'll treat 'em;
> *Frenchmen*, like *storks*, love *frogs*—to eat 'em!"

The alliance, it was patent, was an unholy one, and doomed to disaster.

> Say, *Yankees, don't you feel compunction,*
> At your unnat'ral, rash conjunction?
> Can love for you in him take root,
> Who's Cath-o-lic, and absolute? [43]

Of course not! The Quebec Act had been bad enough, but this cohabitation would be worse, far worse. Granted that France had solemnly sworn that she had no interest in retaking Canada, did anybody in his right mind *believe* that? Ah, the babes, the fools!

Granted that the redcoat was no model of decorum, still you knew where you stood with him.

A Briton, although he loves bottle and wench,
Is an honester fellow than parlez vous French.

Undoubtedly many of the Loyalists believed this, which would help to make it more effective. Undoubtedly many of them felt a genuine fear for the infatuated Whigs. One, John Randolph, who had been the last attorney-general of Virginia—and whose son, Edmund, was to become the first attorney-general of the United States of America—from the Cannon Coffee House, Spring Gardens, London, an exiles' hangout, wrote 25 October 1779 to his friend Thomas Jefferson:

How far the French have been useful to you in Amer, you must be better qualified to determine, than myself; Yet, I cannot avoid expressing my Wish, that you had never enterd into any Engagements with them. They are a people cover'd with Guile, & their Religion countenances the practice of it on all of a different Persuasion. They are educated in an Aversion to the English & hold our Constitution in the utmost Detestation. They have the art to insinuate, & the Wickedness to betray when they gain an admittance. Laws they have none but such as are prescrib'd by the Will of their Prince." [44]

Finally, the good gentleman advised Jefferson, who was governor of Virginia at the time, to "rescind" his Declaration of Independence. Jefferson did not comply with this request.

11

The Inconvenient Aborigines

Americans never have known what to do about the Indians. It was a question that rose before the first colonists started to hew the first trees for clearance of the wilderness; and it is with us still, refusing to go away.

The war that Europeans called the Seven Years War, in America (where in fact it had lasted nine years) was known as the French and Indian War. The English colonists in America had quite naturally linked those two people, who for the most part did work well together. The English colonists didn't understand the redskin, and did not like or trust him, shoving him away as far as possible, and as often. The French colonists, being fewer, and hence more in need of allies, fraternized with the Indians. They learned the Indian languages, which were complicated and many, and they married Indian women, living among the Indians, eating like them, fighting like them, even doing their grotesque war-dances and dedaubing themselves with war-paint, behavior that the English colonists would have found distasteful.

It was in the French and Indian War that George

Washington had heard the zing of bullets for the first time, near Fort Duquesne (which was to become Pittsburgh), and again, under Braddock, on the banks of the Monongahela, both of them slam-bang wilderness battles fought before there had been any proper declaration of war. Almost all of the high-ranking officers of the Continental Army had been subalterns in the French and Indian War—William Heath, John Thomas, Israel Putnam, Seth Pomeroy, Joseph Spencer—and they were heroes in their respective neighborhoods. They were men who had seen War. They had been to another world and could talk in another tongue.

War to the colonial, to most European civilians as well, was a mysterious condition of affairs. It involved a new vocabulary, a whole new set of values. It contained its own laws, which took a heap of learning, and it had nothing to do with the ordinary conduct of life, the humdrum. The men who directed it were looked upon as high priests, and they had only scorn for the uninitiated, those who were *not* the repositories of huge shining secrets. They talked of ravelins and flèches, redans and demilunes, counterscarps, fascines, canister, spontoons, cohorns, whilst moving, eerily, through a world of pipeclay, brass, drum rolls, bugle calls, all the rest of it. They were professionals, and the rest of the world must gawp at them. The red*skins* out in the forest killed men stealthily and in silence. The red*coats* were brave about it, tootling their horns, shouting their commands, doing everything with a clockwork precision. *Theirs* was an intellectual, a civilized form of slaughter, very pretty to behold.

Americans in the French and Indian War had been used largely for labor and for scouting purposes. They could not be trusted in the open, on a field of battle, for they were a slovenly lot, and therefore—it stood to reason—cowards. An American when fired upon dropped to his belly and scrambled behind something, a rock or a tree, before he fired back. What kind of way was that to act?

The colonists themselves wholeheartedly endorsed this opinion, and so helped to spread it. They knew that they were oafs, clowns, and that it would take them a long while to learn how to kill their fellowmen as it should be done. They had seen the French and Indian War start with a series of wild, hysterical, bloody attacks, confusion, panic, and had seen it end, at last, in the proper way, with brilliantly clad soldiers marching upright against one another in serried ranks on the Plains of Abraham and blasting one another down in orderly rows; and there was no question in their minds as to which was the better method. They scoffed at every sugegstion that they take to the bush, that they utilize their knowledge of the wilderness as the Indians did, indulging in what men of a later time would call guerrilla tactics. They accepted the scorn of the European professional. They did not like it, but they accepted it. The parade-ground manner, so hard to acquire, so difficult, obviously was the best.

The trouble was that the Indians didn't know this. The Indians never were to learn. And they were there, always, a weakening people, to be sure, constantly being pushed westward, dependent upon the white man now for their very weapons of war; but they *were* there.

The treaty that ended the Seven Years War was signed in 1763, and the American colonists whooshed in relief. Prosperity beckoned them. Trade with the West Indies, including the slave trade, was on the increase, and peace would increase it even more. True, much of this trade was illegal; but smuggling and associated crimes had long since come to be taken for granted in America. West of the mountains there was that huge sprawling fertile land to be seized bit by luscious bit; and land hunger was endemic among the

Americans. The Indians, to be sure, would have to be pushed back, but this had been done before and could be done again. The Indians always had been a disorganized people, and without somebody behind them, somebody like the French, to supply them with muskets and with powder and ball, they would be negligible, a mere wall of tissue paper. The treaty of peace of 1763 had given all of Canada to Great Britain, so that there was no longer a redman threat from the north. The frontier was wide open, and the colonists surged in that direction.

They were halted, a jerk. Great Britain had won the war, true, but it had been an expensive affair and the nation was deeply in debt, its overtaxed subjects at home clamoring for relief. Great gobs of real estate had been annexed, not only in the New World but in the East as well —for the Seven Years War had been a global war, the first —making the British Empire the biggest in history. This called for protection—more ships, more soldiers. The colonies must help. The British government decided, first off, to eliminate smuggling, to make the customs service not only pay for itself but show a profit, enforcing laws that had been on the books for a long while. Shocked, the Americans howled in protest. It was the beginning of the hard feeling that was to end in revolution. Americans must not only pay customs duties but should pay taxes as well, and the meddlesome men in London began ungracefully to experiment with sundry ill-advised excise laws, which made matters worse.

Thereafter it was to be just a matter of time until the clash came, and the Quebec Act clinched this.

The Quebec Act was passed by Parliament, not without serious opposition, in 1774, at just about the same time as the so-called Intolerable Acts that were designed to punish Boston for the Tea Party. Most Americans, perhaps all of them, believed that it *was* one of the Intolerable Acts, and they thought it the most obnoxious of all. The Quebec Act, in fact, had been framed by a totally different committee, and only after long and careful consideration of the whole Canadian situation. It was farseeing, statesmanlike, broadminded; but its wording was hardly diplomatic, and its timing was, to say the least of it, maladroit.

The Quebec Act imposed the British criminal law upon Canada but permitted the old French civil law. It went further. It recognized the Roman Catholic Church and established Canadian Catholics—well over nine-tenths of the population—as equal subjects, freer than the Catholics of Great Britain, who still were under many restrictions. To the average American, and especially to the nearby New Englander, this was putting everything right back to where it had been before the war. It meant that the menacing force to the north had not been removed at all, but legitimatized.

More, in an effort to protect the rights of the Indians—who in the eyes of the Americans *had* no rights—the Quebec Act extended Canada south of the Great Lakes to the Ohio River. That is, it blocked off all of what was then beginning to be called the Northwest Territory—the present states of Ohio, Indiana, Michigan, Illinois, and Wisconsin—and declared this to be Indian property forever.

Several colonies—Massachusetts, Pennsylvania, Connecticut, Virginia—claimed big chunks of this land and had made plans to subdivide and sell it. Many companies had been formed for this purpose, much money invested. Now, without any conference with the residents of the coastal colonies, all this was to be given, willy-nilly, to that dirty, treacherous, bloodthirsty heathen, the redskin.

An intolerable act, indeed!

If the colonists never did know what to do about the Indians this was no more than natural, for the Indians never knew what to do about themselves. It was their greatest weakness that they could not act together. They were broken up into hundreds and even thousands of tribes and sub-tribes, none of them stable, all mercurial. Two groups might get together and form a war party, but the chances were that they would separate before the fighting started, and even in the event of a victory they would not stay together long enough to press their advantage but would fall to squabbling about the spoils. Tribes sometimes conferred, but they seldom put into action anything that they might chance to agree on. They had no treaties, in the western sense of the word, for they were illiterate; and whatever general understandings they sometimes adopted they soon broke. Much of the time they could not even confer intelligibly, for they had many languages and dialects and of course no writing, so that often the Indians in one valley could not understand a word spoken by those in the next valley. They had no one religion, no one set of beliefs, to bind them. They did not even possess, as did the widely scattered Polynesians, a single *set* of gods, howsoever amorphous, howsoever varied.

Pushing such people around had not been hard. Some of the tribes were so small that they could not exist alone and were obliged to combine with strangers. Some were so sickly that they were dying out: smallpox, in particular, wiped away great numbers of them. *Individually* they might make fine fighters, but whenever two or more of them got together there was sure to be confusion and uncertainty of purpose.

True, Pontiac had brought together, briefly, the Ottawa, the Ojibwa, the Potawatomi; but Pontiac was a genius, and geniuses, always rare, were rarest of all among the red men.

At the time of the American Revolution, however, the west-planning colonists were confronted with two formidable exceptions to this rule of disunity, one at the northern end of the line, one at the southern.

The Creek Confederation, though its name tended to make it seem more redoubtable than in fact it was, for the Indians was a miracle of get-togetherness. It had no central ruler or ruling body; it operated upon no fixed principle; and it continued to exist largely because there was nobody to try to smash it. The confederation was made up of the Chickasaw, the smallest tribe, the most friendly to the Americans; the Cherokee, the most nearly civilized; the Choctaw, a sullen but lazy people; and the Creeks, the most numerous, the most widespread, and the fiercest, who were in close touch with both the Spaniards to the west and south and the Americans to the east. Among them they could have put close to fourteen thousand braves into the field at one time; but they never did. They did not fight against one another; but neither did they often fight *with* one another, side by side, like brothers.

There were smaller subtribes and breakoffs, some of which, like the Timucua, the Calusa, and the Apalachee Indians east of the mountains, and also, there, the Powhatans and the Nanticokes, had simply and quietly ceased to exist. The Natchez, for example. The Natchez might have numbered four thousand at one time, and though they talked a Muskogean dialect they had certain customs of their own, different from those of their neighbors: they flattened their babies' heads, for instance, and they maintained a rigid caste society. The Natchez had offended the early French settlers along the Mississippi, who massacred them, virtually wiping them out.

The Chickamaugas were theoretically a sept of the Cherokee, but in truth they were highly independent in their habits. A scrappy group, though small, they could not be depended upon.

The Seminoles were a Creek tribe that had broken off entirely and had taken up residence in the peninsula of East Florida, where many of them still live.

The Creeks themselves were split into Northern and Southern Creeks, which must be dealt with separately.

The Creeks, speaking of them by and large, were slightly less savage than most of the Indians with whom the Atlantic coastal settlers had made contact, and slightly more intelligent. They might take a scalp now and then, but they did not glory in hideous torture like the tribesmen farther north. They dabbled in agriculture, but only on a small scale, and hunting remained their chief manner of life. Since they had forgotten how to make their own bows and arrows, their own tomahawks and spears, they had come to depend upon the musket, which made them dependent upon the white man for supplies. They did not, generally, trust the Americans, whom they believed to be greedy for their lands, but neither did they trust the Spaniards, who tried to keep them stirred up against the men from the coast, to use them as a buffer. All they had to sell was furs and hides, and they carried on this trade almost entirely through Scots, who in the vast forests south of the Ohio River mixed with the aborigines very much as had the French in the forests north of that river.

At the time of the Revolution the mountains screened off most of the Creeks from the coastal colonists, especially those in Virginia and the Carolinas. In Georgia it was different. There was no mountain barrier for the Georgians, who buzzed with rumors to the effect that the British-stirred-up Creeks were about to come sweeping down upon them, so that they were reluctant to send their own fighting men north to aid the Continental cause.

One thing that even the Georgians were willing to grant the Creeks: they did not give refuge to runaway

slaves, as so many other Indians did. There was no tempta-
tion for blacks in bondage to scamper for shelter to the
Creek country; for the Creeks accepted the white man's
institution *in toto,* keeping any blacks that came their way
as working prisoners, a lot exactly like the one that they
had left. Thus, Alexander McGillivray, the greatest chief of
them all—he was half Scottish, a quarter French, a quarter
Creek—and James Colbert (French-Scottish-Chickasaw) and
also William McIntosh (Creek-Scotch) had slaves to do the
hard work on their plantations in the very midst of the
wilderness. McGillivray at one time kept as many as sixty
of these.

No adulterine but a full-blooded Scot, a descendant in
the royal line forsooth, John Stuart was His Majesty's Commissioner of Indian Affairs south of the Ohio. He was rough-
mouthed, and there was nothing conciliatory about him.
He was indeed a highly irascible man, given to sulfurous
outpourings. He couldn't have spoken with forked tongue
if he tried, and perhaps this is why the Indians, who sensed
this, trusted him. Aristocrat though he was, he could mix
with them, sleeping in their tents, eating their food, but he
never did take unto himself any Indian wife or wives, and
he preferred to live east of the mountains, where he could
call for clean linen and for cooled wine. He had once been
a prisoner of the Cherokee, condemned to death, but had
been saved by a high chief, Attakullakulla ("Little Car-
penter"), whose friendship, which stayed, influenced the rest
of his career. John Stuart was a disagreeable man,[45] but he
really had the interests of his dusky charges at heart, and
when the last royal governor of South Carolina, Lord William Campbell, ordered him to kick up a border war for
the purpose of embarrassing the Patriots, he flatly refused.
He was a servant of the King, sir, but such a war would
soon get out of hand, and it would be as hard on the

Loyalists as on the rebels. Campbell fumed; but Stuart stood firm. Campbell, engulfed by Patriots, had to skip the province, never to return. John Stuart, no doubt blaspheming to the end, died in bed in Charleston, 1779, and the southern states were spared the horrors of border warfare.

In the north the situation was entirely different. There the Iroquois had formed an organization that made the Creeks' organization look childish.

Two misty figures, Deganawida, a Huron, and Hiawatha,[46] an Onondaga born, both of them adopted into the Mohawk tribe, by means of nobody will ever know what prodigious labors and coaxings, had consolidated the five principal tribes in what is now New York State, besides western New England, western Pennsylvania, and even a part of southern Canada. These were, from east to west: the Senecas, Cayugas, Onondagas, Oneidas, and Mohawks. Together they were known as the Iroquois. They had a polysyllabic jargon of their own to describe their grouping, a real jawbreaker, but to the Dutch and the later English they were quite naturally known as the Five Nations.

They were famous fighters, and by the simple process of sticking together they easily defeated their neighbors— the previously powerful Huron, Neutrals, Eries, and, to the south, the Susquehannocks, including the Conestogas. They controlled the important Mohawk Valley, the land that stretched between Niagara and the little lakes on the west, the upper reaches of the Hudson on the east; and this meant that they very largely controlled the whole fur trade.

The Iroquois were possessed of an insensate cruelty. They could kill a captive all night long, on specially built torture platforms, and the entire community would turn out to witness the affair, as in more benign countries and among less murderous people communities might turn out *en masse* of a summer night to hear a band concert. The most ferocious of them all were the ones farthest east, the Mohawks, who had the loose, weak, sickly tribes of New England terrified, and who collected tribute from these simply by threat of a visit. The Mohawks, since they *were* the easternmost of the Iroquois, were the first to come into contact with the white man. They were the first to get firearms. A Mohawk, to any European, whether in Europe or visiting in America, was the very epitome of the red savage. The others were not modeled after the Mohawks, but they seemed so to newcomers.

Early in the eighteenth century another tribe, the Tuscaroras, came north from the Carolina country to join the Iroquois confederation, which thereafter was to be known as the *Six* Nations. The Tuscaroras lived in western New York State. They still do.

The undisputed leader of the Six Nations, the most powerful chief of them all, was an Irishman. It was he who kept the Iroquois on the British side when all of the other redskins were siding with the friendlier French.

William Johnson came to America at the age of twenty-three for the purpose of managing some estates just south of the Mohawk River that his uncle, Captain Peter Warren, R.N., a man in line to become an admiral, and who, moreover, had married into the De Lancey family of New York. The lad soon took these estates off his uncle's hands, and he bought or was given a great deal of nearby acreage as well. He learned the language of the Iroquois, their various dialects, all the way from the Berkshires to Niagara Falls. He presided over their councils. He settled their affairs. He was honest with them, something no other white trader had thought to be. He had three children by his indentured servant Catherine Weisenberg and married her on her deathbed. She was a white woman. He never did marry any of the various Indian women he took into his household from time to time, the most important of these being Caroline, a niece of the Mohawk chief Hendrick, by whom he had three children, and Molly, or Mary, sister to Joseph Brant, another Six Nations chief, whose real name was Thayendanegea, by whom he had eight.

William Johnson was stupendous, a giant. With a whistle he could summon thousands of scowling warriors. The Indians called him Warraghiyagey, whatever that meant. The British made him a major general, and after his victories in the Seven Years War a baronet—*Sir* William Johnson. He was appointed Superintendent of Indian Affairs north of the Ohio, the northern equivalent of John Stuart, though he was a much more powerful personage than Stuart. He owned more land than he would ever be able to pace. He built a stone mansion just north of the present Johnstown—it is still there—and he built many frontier forts, which he garrisoned and which he commanded. He died in 1772, leaving his house, his title, and most of his real estate to John Johnson, his son by Catherine Weisenberg, though his half-caste offspring were not forgotten.

At the outbreak of the American Revolution there was a considerable scramble to enlist the services or at least ensure the neutrality of the Iroquois. The Iroquois were not what they had been a little earlier, for whiskey and warfare alike had taken their toll, but they were still a formidable force, and they still sat astride the Mohawk Valley, which would not, like the valley of the St. Lawrence a little farther north, become impassable in winter.

Each side in the Revolution loudly insisted that it would not enlist savages, who, it had been established, could not be prevented, in victory, from scalping and otherwise mutilating prisoners who were still alive. Burke stormed against the practice for three and a half hours in the Commons; and Pitt did the same in the Lords; but these magnificent orations did not change a single vote, and in America the representatives of the King went right on offer-

ing the redskins beads, mirrors, red cloth, rum. Perhaps the
Patriots would have done the same thing if they'd been
given a chance. They did sign on a few scattered groups,
such as the Stockbridge Indians of Massachusetts, an effete
and vanishing people, but these hardly counted. The Loyalists, thanks largely to the heirs of Sir William Johnson, of
whatever pigmentation, got the Iroquois.

The best that the Patriots could do, in Tryon County,
New York, was to persuade the Onondagas and some of the
Senecas to stay out of the war, at least for a little while.

Sir John Johnson, the head of the family, though forced
to flee to Canada after Burgoyne's splashy failure in the
Lake Champlain–Lake George country, was able to raise a
Loyalist regiment. The Royal Yorkers, they called themselves; but they were more commonly known, because of the
color of their coats, as Johnson's Greens. Based on the large
British post of Niagara, they employed Indians, and they
specialized in hit-and-run raids, leaving behind them the
ashes of Patriot houses and the hairless bodies of farmers,
their wives, and their children. The fighting in the Mohawk
Valley was rather more than just another "little war," with
neighbor pitted against neighbor. It was rather a war of its
own, and a singularly bitter one. With the Cherry Valley
massacre, which could be called its high point—or low point
—it caused the Continental commanders to realize that the
Iroquois must be stamped out, once and for all.

The Patriots never had given up hope of conquering
Canada. When Montgomery was killed and Benedict Arnold
badly hurt before Quebec, which marked the end of *that*
double-speared attack upon the northern land, the Continentals still hopefully girded their loins, watching for a
second chance. Troops were actually massed for invasion
purposes near Albany, troops put in charge of the Marquis
de Lafayette, of all persons. This expedition never did take

off. There was too much to do at home. However, Washington authorized Major General John Sullivan to see that Tryon County was stripped.

Sullivan was a New Hampshire lawyer who never seemed to have good luck as a soldier. He did everything that he was supposed to do, and he served throughout the Revolution, but his efforts never were sprinkled with success.

The war was getting along. It was early in May of 1779 that Sullivan began to assemble in Pennsylvania, in the valley of the Susquehanna, the forty-five hundred men allotted to him. What with troubles about supplies and the usual bickering about promotions, it was late August before this huge force—the British could not possibly have matched it, and did not try to—started north. By that time, of course, the Finger Lakes country had been alerted.

Had Sullivan knocked out the fort at Niagara it might have made a big difference in the conduct of the war and perhaps even have cleared the way for that long-wished-for conquest of Canada. But he didn't even threaten Niagara. Instead he thudded up through the Seneca country and the Cayuga country, burning deserted villages, fighting only now and then, when he had to, and winning easily enough, for his forces were overwhelmingly superior. He lost only about forty men of his own, from all causes, and seized or destroyed some 160,000 bushels of corn besides uncountable other foodstuffs. He went as far west as Gathtsecwardhare on the Genesee, and then, cumbrously, he returned.

The winter that followed was to·prove the harshest in memory. Sullivan's ponderous and expensive movement had not proved anything and had not damaged in any way the Loyalist forces under Sir John Johnson, who simply stayed out of his way. But it had taken the heart out of the Iroquois confederation. It had ended the sovereignty of the Six Nations.

12

"The Heart Which Is Conscious of Its Own Rectitude"

THE INTERNECINE NATURE OF THIS WAR was never clearer than in the environs of New York City shortly after that port had been taken by General Howe, who had come from Boston by way of Halifax with a huge army of redcoats and German mercenaries in the largest fleet that ever the world had seen—much larger, in men, guns, and bottoms, than the vaunted Spanish Armada. Howe had had no trouble taking Manhattan Island, for the untrained Continentals ran at the first growl. His troubles began when he had to find a way to feed his men.

The British soldier wanted fresh meat, preferably beef. He believed that he needed this to keep up his strength. His officers, for their part, wanted to see that he got, as well, fresh vegetables and fresh fruit, for this was the only way in which they could stave off scurvy, a debilitating disease that seldom killed but laid up men in large numbers, and to which the soldiers were just as liable as were sailors at sea, provided they were kept on a diet of salted food. The fleet could keep the salted stuff coming; but the surrounding countryside must be searched for fresh provisions, since the farms on Manhattan itself were few and small.

Staten Island gave no trouble. It was the first place taken, and it was easily retained throughout the war. But it had little livestock, and the products of its gardens could have been wolfed by the British Army in one sitting.

Staten Island, parenthetically, was best known to the Continentals as the place where the British maintained their money-making machines, their presses. These had been aboard the frigate *Phoenix* in the early days of the blockade, before Howe got there from Nova Scotia, but they were soon moved to the island, where throughout the war they continued to turn out expertly designed counterfeit colonial money, the first time, it is believed, that this particular weapon of warfare was used, though it was not to be the last.[47] This, together with the colonies' tendency to issue unbacked paper money of their own, so drove down the value of Congressional notes that the phrase "not worth a Continental" was born.

Congress had issued $6,000,000 in paper money in 1775, $19,000,000 in 1776, $13,000,000 in 1777, more than $63,000,000 in 1778, and $140,000,000 in 1779. At the end of 1777 the dollar was worth 33 cents; at the beginning of 1779 it was worth 12 cents; from the beginning of 1780 the value was less than 2 cents. Some extraordinary price tags resulted. In 1780 General Gates came out of semi-retirement in Virginia to take over the Army of the South, then in South Carolina, and Congress allowed him $30,000 travel expenses, though the distance was not great. Jefferson had to pay $355.50 for three bottles of brandy, Thomas Paine $300 for a pair of *woolen* stockings, and John Witherspoon, the president of Princeton, $1,000 for a coat that didn't fit. George Washington's expenses were, understandably, enormous. The commander-in-chief had volunteered to serve without pay, but like the good housekeeper that he was he kept careful tabs on his outpayments, and he turned in the whole bill after the war had ended and when those inflated prices were at an all-time high, a fact gleefully noted by the author of a recent best-selling book, who managed to make the Father of His Country look like a cheat.

Long Island was larger and every bit as secure, and its cabbages and potatoes, its chicken and pigs and cows, went to the redcoats, who, to give them credit, paid cash. There were sometimes raids from out of Connecticut ports across the Sound, but for the most part Long Island was untouched by the war, so that Nathan Hale, in civilian clothes, having come over from Connecticut, could travel much of the length of the island, making military notes, before, quite by chance, he was recognized—and hanged.

Hale was made much of, for the Continental cause badly needed a hero at that time. Only a few months before his hanging, Moses Dunbar of Wallingford, Connecticut, another young man of the same rank, captain, had been caught recruiting for a Loyalist outfit in Hartford—he had made only one convert, a man whose name was John Adams!—and despite his youth, his pretty wife, his four small children, and the fact that there was no law against recruiting for the Loyalist cause in Connecticut at that time (but the legislature quickly took care of that, passing one that was retroactive), he was hanged. The spot has not been marked.[48] Statues have been erected to Nathan Hale, but there are no statues of Moses Dunbar. He had picked the wrong side. How could a Tory be a martyr?

Northern New Jersey, and especially Bergen County, and most especially the valley of the Hackensack River, were mixed. There were farmers in those parts who were delighted to carry good fresh food into New York City, accepting cash for it, perhaps accepting also, and for nothing, a great fistful of counterfeit money, which the British gave away to anybody who would carry it out into the countryside. These men were willing to run little errands for the British, spreading false reports, counting the Continental troops at this outpost or at that. There were others who opposed such activities—and opposed them musket in hand, or perhaps with a torch, for barn burnings were common and murder from ambush by no means unknown. Like all such "little wars" the Hackensack Valley contest was bitter, unforgiving, and seemed to get worse as time went on. Neighbors cursed one another, hated one another, and sometimes hanged or shot one another, all in the name of patriotism.

Worst of all was Westchester County, New York, just north of the city. The territory east of the Hudson between the British positions at the north of the city and the Continental positions in the Highlands, roughly thirty miles north and south, was called the Neutral Ground. It could have been called no-man's land. It included most of Westchester County, and was a good place to stay away from.

The Cowboys and the Skinners fought one another back and forth across the Neutral Ground, and their fighting was not pretty.

The Cowboys [49] specialized in getting cattle by whatever method was most convenient, usually theft, and they drove these down to the Yonkers line, where they could be sold to British quartermasters and no questions asked.

The Skinners specialized in intercepting the Cowboys and stealing their cattle from them. They might sell these cattle to the Continentals of the Highlands or they might kill them and skin them out, selling the hides and the meat separately.

The Skinners and the Cowboys were classified by both armies as "irregular militia." A better word would have been bandits.

It was three Skinners on a routine patrol the muggy

morning of Saturday, 23 September 1780, who performed all unwittingly one of the most notable acts of the war.

The three were stationed at a small bridge at the north end of the village of Tarrytown. They were John Paulding, a huge man, David Williams, and Isaac Van Wart. This was on the White Plains road, and it was in territory which, though part of the Neutral Ground, had been traversed many times by the Cowboys. It was for this reason, and also because the New York legislature recently had passed a law providing that the "volunteer militiamen" could keep the personal possessions of any such prisoners as they might make, provided that these could be proved to be Loyalist, that they were keeping a sharp lookout.

It was some time between nine and ten o'clock that a horseman came in sight, from the north, making in the direction of White Plains—and New York City. He was wearing a long blue cloak, and seemed to be carrying no sword or any other weapon, certainly not a musket. He wore a round hat, not cocked. He must have been a civilian.

The Skinners carried muskets, but they wore no sort of uniform or badge or insignia of office. The bridge was a narrow one, and they blocked it effectively. The traveler did not seem disconcerted, but rather was pleased, and from the way he talked to them about pushing on to the city they gathered that he thought that they were Cowboys. When he learned his mistake he fished out a piece of paper which he declared was a let-pass signed by General Arnold, the Patriot commander of that whole military district from Fishkill down to Tarrytown.

The only one of the Skinners who could read was the oldest, the giant Paulding, and he examined the paper. He pronounced it a let-pass all right, and it was certainly signed Benedict Arnold, though Paulding could not answer for the handwriting, since he had never had any dealings with the

Capture of Major André

hero-general. The let-pass, Paulding reported, described the holder as John Anderson, a New York merchant.

There was something fishy here. The Skinners, their minds on that new law that in effect made land privateers of them, ordered the stranger into the bushes, where they made him strip to the buff. By this time he was offering them all sorts of money—to be paid later, it must be assumed —for letting him go on to New York City; but they gave no mind to this.

They were disappointed in what they found. The man had no pistol, no sword, and almost no money, a few coppers; and the only piece of jewelry he carried was his watch, a fairly good one; but this, assuming that the fellow was indeed a legitimate prisoner, would have to be divided not only among the three captors but also and equally among the four other members of the patrol, who were not presently in sight but could be summoned at any moment.

They did find, tight in between his ankles and his stockings, six sheets of paper upon which words and figures had been written in a hand that, Paulding averred, was the same as the hand in which the let-pass had been written. This looked very strange. They permitted the man to dress, and then, despite his voluble objections, they took him to the nearest Continental Army post, which was at North Castle, and turned him over to Lieutenant Colonel John Jameson, after which they went back to the bridge north of Tarrytown, hoping for better luck with the next wayfarer.

Jameson had had no experience with intelligence work, and his second-in-command, Major Benjamin Tallmadge, who had, was absent. The sheets of paper taken from the prisoner certainly were written in General Arnold's own hand, which Jameson knew. And they did seem to be plans of West Point, up the river a little, and of certain outworks, together with lists of the scattered Continental troops.

I *Benedict Arnold Major General*
do acknowledge the UNITED STATES of AME-
RICA to be Free, Independent and Sovereign States, and
declare that the people thereof owe no allegiance or obedience to George the Third, King of Great-Britain; and I
renounce, refuſe and abjure any allegiance or obedience to
him; and I do   *Swear*   that I will, to the ut-
moſt of my power, ſupport, maintain and defend the ſaid
United States againſt the ſaid King George the Third, his
heirs and ſucceſſors, and his or their abettors, aſſiſtants and
adherents, and will ſerve the ſaid United States in the office of
Major General   which I now hold, with
fidelity, according to the beſt of my ſkill and underſtanding.

Sworn before me this   *B Arnold*
30th. May 1778 at the
Artillery Park Valley Forge *Henry B Elah*

*The Oath of Allegiance to the United States, signed by Benedict
Arnold at Valley Forge, 1778*

Jameson had been notified by the general—as had all other post commanders in the vicinity—to watch out for and admit through the lines promptly a civilian named John Anderson who would come from New York. That order, however, had been sent three days ago, and this prisoner, this Anderson, if he was Anderson, had come not from the direction of the city but from the north. Also, the order, like the let-pass, was written in Benedict Arnold's own hand, though ordinarily such work would be done by one of the general's aides, Major David Franks or Lieutenant Colonel Richard Varick, both of whom Jameson knew were with the general at the Robinson mansion, his headquarters, a little downriver from West Point and on the east bank.[50]

The whole thing was made even more complicated by the fact that General Washington himself, together with several of his high-ranking staff officers, were expected at the Robinson mansion the very next morning for breakfast on their way back from a Hartford, Connecticut, conference with the top French generals from Newport, Rhode Island. If there was some sort of plot to seize West Point and thus smash the whole Continental center it could include in its stroke the commander-in-chief himself, who of course would have suspected nothing, West Point being in the hands of so reliable a soldier as Benedict Arnold. Moreover, if the British were going to strike upriver this would be their time. The wind was strong and steady from the south, perfect for their purposes.

Jameson thought of turning over the whole matter to the commander-in-chief, who should be at the Robinson house for breakfast tomorrow. On the other hand, General Arnold, a stocky swart man, a darkly handsome disagreeable man, was a stern commander and not one easily bypassed. Arnold would not be mild in his treatment of a subordinate who tried to go over his head.

Jameson solved his problem, as he thought, by sending

messengers to *both* men, the one to Arnold carrying news of the capture of "John Anderson" and asking what should be done with him, the one to Washington containing the captured papers. The Washington messenger had farther to go, for he was expected to intercept the commander-in-chief on the way south from Danbury, where according to plans Washington, always an early riser, would spend the night. The messenger to General Arnold had to go only as far as the Robinson house. However, the messenger to Washington was much better mounted, and Jameson reasonably supposed that they would reach their respective goals at about the same time. He wasn't to know—nobody could have known— that Washington on the way from Hartford would run into the French minister, De La Luzerne, who would talk him and his companions into spending the night with him, instead, at Fishkill, a little farther north. Thence in fact the whole party had gone—the commander-in-chief, his aide, a youngster named Alexander Hamilton, and his companions, Major General the Marquis de Lafayette, and Brigadier General Henry Knox, chief of artillery of the Continental Army, together with *their* aides.

At the last moment the prisoner, when he learned what was going on, asked if he might send a message to General Washington; and this request Colonel Jameson granted. The prisoner explained that he was not "John Anderson" at all but John André, major in the British Army, adjutant general to Sir Henry Clinton in charge of intelligence. He had been tricked into this "humiliating" position behind the American lines, he complained, and was not in uniform, but he was sure that General Washington would understand. General Washington did—once he had received the letter. The well-mounted messenger chased him all the way to Danbury in vain, and then doubled back, so that he did not reach the commander-in-chief until the middle of the afternoon.

The wind was still from the south.

Benedict Arnold

Benedict Arnold had recived *his* letter, telling him that "John Anderson" had been taken prisoner, as he was about to sit down to breakfast with his own aides and those of the southcoming generals, who had ridden ahead. He never ate that meal. Leaving his wife and baby, he lit out for the British lines, where he surrendered himself together with his unsullied sword. Specifically, he went to the armed sloop *Vulture,* riding at anchor off Verplanck's Point, some fourteen miles downriver.

The wind had swung around, and now was coming from the north. It started to rain.

In a cabin aboard the *Vulture,* Major General Arnold was writing an excuse-it-please note to his chief:

> The heart which is conscious of its own rectitude, cannot attempt to palliate a step which the world may censure as wrong; I have ever acted from a principle of love to my country, since the commencement of the present unhappy contest between Great Britain and the Colonies . . .

That phrase "the present unhappy contest," or, as it often appeared, "the present unnatural contest," was common to letters written by Loyalists and Patriots alike; but it was most favored by the Loyalists.

> . . . the same principle of love to my country actuates my present conduct, however, it may appear inconsistent to the world, who very seldom judge right of any man's actions.

The letter is a little masterpiece, hypocrisy personified on paper, a very *cri de coeur,* if a traitor can be said to have a heart.

"And now whom can we trust?" said Washington, when he had read it.

Benedict Arnold didn't lose by this deal. He saw to that. The British made him only a brigadier general, who had been a proud major general in the Continental Army, but the brigadiership paid £200 a year. He was also given the colonelcy of a regiment that paid £450 a year, besides perquisites; and Arnold had a deft hand with a perquisite. His wife, perhaps because she swooned so readily, on command, like a dog rolling over, was given a pension of £500 a year. The British gave the traitor various dirty jobs to do, and he did them very well, for he was an excellent military man, perhaps the best tactician, the best *battlefield operator*, in either army. His three small sons were given British Army commissions, sinecures, each of which was worth about £225 a year. Papa of course pocketed that.

He did all right for himself. He also won an imperishable place in the annals of infamy.

André? He was hanged. David Williams, Isaac Van Wart, and John Paulding were allowed, by a military court, his horse, bridle, saddle, and watch; but they had to share these with the four unnamed associates, men who had not actually participated in the arrest, which caused them to grumble much.

The Patriots of the time were wont to point at Benedict Arnold as a prize specimen of the species Loyalist. This is unfair. It was no sudden prodding on the part of Satan that had prompted his sellout. He had not been carried away by a gust of emotion. He had planned the business for at least a year and a half, as the records show. The British did not sneak up behind him, whispering honeyed promises. *He* went to *them*. He proposed the betrayal, proposing the price as well; and when the other side faltered, he bolstered its determination, refusing to let the treacherous proposal die.

He haggled shamelessly over the terms—so much for each prisoner, so much for each ton of surrendered gunpowder and so on. He had asked George Washington for the West Point assignment, and when Washington suggested that he be given command of the right flank of the forthcoming movement on Yorktown—the post of honor, the sort of place he would have jumped at a little earlier—he pleaded that his left leg, wounded before Quebec three years ago, and again at Saratoga, would not permit this.[51] He kept his eye on the booty all the while.

It was true that General Arnold, while military commander of Philadelphia, a post that permitted plenty of jiggling with perquisites, was married to Peggy Shippen, who came of a Loyalist family and had expensive tastes; but there is no reason to believe that she egged him on, though neither did she do anything to thwart him.

It is true too that Arnold first opened the correspondence with General Clinton's adjutant by means of a couple of prominent Tories, Joseph Stansbury of Philadelphia and the Reverend Jonathan Odell, temporarily of New York. This did not mean that he proposed to join their party, in which he had never expressed the faintest interest. He was no starry-eyed idealist. He was just a crook.

The Loyalists of the American Revolution have enough to answer for when they are arraigned before the bar of history. They should be spared Benedict Arnold.

13

Nightmare in Newburgh

THE WAR had been going on for six years when Cornwallis surrendered his army at Yorktown. It might then be supposed that George Washington, who had been through the whole horrid business, had endured every moment of the agony, would be able to relax, lean back, take things easy for a while. This was not so. There was to be no rest for the weary commander-in-chief.

The two nations no longer were fighting; but they were still at war, and until they had agreed upon a peace Washington must keep his tatterdemalion army together, somehow, lest the British in one fell swoop undo all that had been done over the long bitter years. Patching up a peace might take a long while. Three thousand miles of Atlantic brine remained in place, slowing everything. There were problems —fishing rights off the Grand Banks, indemnity for slaves seized as contraband, relocation and return of the prisoners on both sides, and worst of all indemnity for the confiscation of Loyalist property, something that the British insisted upon. The news from Paris, where the delegates were meeting, was spotty.

British surrender at Yorktown

Keeping the Continental Army together always had been a Herculean task. It was harder now than ever. Even if a peace *was* agreed upon, the men could not be disbanded until they had been paid; and how were they to be paid? Men in the ranks muttered about mutiny always a possibility in that force, a downright likelihood now.

Washington had established his headquarters at Newburgh, on the Hudson some sixty miles above New York City. There he existed from day to day, serene to see, inwardly in turmoil. The supply situation, what with the British grabbing everything they could reach in that district, was more critical than ever before. There was no longer any hope of glory to dangle before the men, who wanted to go home but of course insisted upon being paid first.

Washington himself had been a member of Congress, which in 1775 had appointed him commander-in-chief of the newly formed Continental Army. A conscientious man, and not unaware of the American public's aversion to militarism, he had been careful to defer to Congress the governing body in all matters that might call for a political solution. He still did this, after Yorktown; but it was no longer the same Congress. It had degenerated, as newcomers pushed forward while old-time patriots retired to their home states in order to take up affairs that they esteemed of much greater importance—Patrick Henry, for example, resigned from the Congress to become the first governor of an independent Virginia—or, like Washington himself, got into the active campaigning. The original assemblage had been a noteworthy one—upright men, honest men, sincerely concerned with the welfare of the new nation they were helping to create. The Congress in 1781 was a noisy group of favor-seekers, ambitious lawyers, pettifoggers. Under its ministrations the currency of the country had become so debased as to be worthless even as souvenirs; and Congress no longer even had any of *that* to appropriate. Yet Washington was obliged—or thought himself obliged, in order to choke off the cry of military dictatorship, another Cromwell—still to treat them as gentlemen.

It was in the midst of this that there came crashing down upon him, like a load of bricks tilted from out of a dumpcart, the Huddy affair.

Washington always had hated and feared the Loyalists. He was essentially a moderate man, a careful man, and never vindictive; but he could not damn the Tories often enough or savagely enough. And now he was given added reason for these curses.

New Jersey, always a cantankerous state, in the beginning of the conflict had been esteemed a largely Loyalist district; but nobody seemed certain of this, and the popular favor wobbled from side to side. General Howe had been disappointed in the response to his offer of a statement of loyalty to all residents of New Jersey who would swear allegiance to the King. Those who *did* this—not in the large numbers that the general had expected—in their turn were disappointed. They repudiated the pledges, which they declared did not insure them against looting. The redcoats either were illiterate or pretended to be, brushing the "protections" aside, whereas the Hessians, famous predators, could not read English. This experiment, which made for a lot of hard feeling on both sides, had been written down as a failure; and after Trenton and Princeton, anyway, the need for it had evaporated.

Of all the "little wars" that were an unfortunate feature of the American Revolution—the venomous, split-neighborhood affairs—one of the worst was that which raged in Monmouth County, New Jersey, between the Retaliators, or Patriots, and the King's Bravoes, sometimes called the Pine Robbers.

Joshua Huddy was a Patriot, but not a Retaliator. He was an army man, a captain in the Continental forces, and he had been in charge of a small lookout post at Dover, New Jersey,[52] in March of 1782 when it was overrun by the British in a lightning raid. Huddy, a captive, was thrown into one of the British naval hulks, prison ships, in New York harbor, a fate generally considered to be much worse than death. He did not stay there long.

Huddy had been harsh, it seemed. Among other things he had hanged a prisoner of his, Stephen Edwards, a Monmouth County neighbor and a Loyalist. There were many who never forgave him for this, though it was a common practice on both sides. He was also blamed for the death of a Monmouth County carpenter-turned-privateer, Philip White, a man who had been from the beginning a staunch Loyalist. White was taken off Long Branch the morning of March 30, and by the time he reached Monmouth Court House he was no more than a corpse. The Patriots said he had resisted arrest, the Loyalists that he had been murdered in cold blood. Whatever the truth, and despite the fact that this was six days after the capture and imprisonment of Huddy, it was Huddy who was blamed for the death.

There had recently been formed in New York City the Board of Associated Loyalists, an effort to regularize the "irregular militia" groups of Loyalists that operated unpredictably in New Jersey as they did in Westchester County. The head of this board, and its chief organizer, was William Franklin, the Loyalist son of Benjamin Franklin, who had once been governor of New Jersey but had been booted out by the victorious Patriots, imprisoned in Connecticut, then the American Siberia, and only recently released in an exchange. Ex-Governor Franklin, as a civilian, and the bearer of a famous name, was supposed to lend the board respectability, but the arrangement it had made with Sir Henry Clinton, the British commander-in-chief in New York City, did not suggest any official trust of the new body. Clinton, in truth, never had any faith in any of the Loyalists.

The Franklins were a badly split family. The ex-governor was himself a bastard—though Benjamin Franklin had stoutly refused to name the mother—and *his* son, William Temple Franklin, was also a bastard, the illegitimate son of an illegitimate father. To complicate matters, William Temple Franklin, scarcely more than a boy, was a Patriot, and was at this very time acting as his grandfather's secretary in the peace talks in Paris.

The ex-governor, thinking, mistakenly, that he had done a fine thing when he gave his blessing to the Board of Associated Loyalists, sailed for England to join the émigrés of the Adelphi in the Strand. He was lucky. He had nothing to do with the Huddy affair.

Richard Lippincott was a Loyalist militia captain, another Monmouth County man, and a person of some consequence there, being married indeed to a Borden of Bordentown. It was he who was given the order, by his proper superior, to take Joshua Huddy out of the prison hulk and carry him back to Monmouth County, presumably in exchange for some British officer who was a prisoner of the rebels, though this person was not named. Lippincott took this order to the commander-in-chief, this being a proviso in Sir Henry's arrangement with the Associated Loyalists. Clinton, seeing nothing wrong with it, signed it.

Lippincott and his men did take Huddy back to Monmouth County, specifically to Sandy Hook, but they did not exchange him. Instead, they suspended around his neck a sign reading "We, the Refugees, having long with grief beheld the cruel murders of our brethren . . . determine to hang man for man while there is a Refugee existing." Then, in larger letters: "Up Goes Huddy for Philip White." And they strangled him.

This was too much. There was hell to pay at Monmouth Court House. Sunday, 15 April, three days after the lynching, the Reverend John Woodhull, a Presbyterian, speaking from the steps of the inn—the church could not hold the crowd— gave forth a fiery eye-for-an-eye-tooth-for-a-tooth sermon, after which more than four hundred persons signed what soon came to be known as the Monmouth Manifesto. A copy of this was sent to General Washington. Newburgh was only about a hundred miles away, as the crow flies, but the military situation near New York City being what it was it took five days for the Manifesto to get there.

What it amounted to was that the signees pledged themselves, if Huddy's death was not avenged, to break away from the conventional Patriot cause and go to war against the British and the Loyalists by themselves—openly.

Washington could not possibly afford to let this happen. His army, teetering on the brink of dissolution, would have fallen to pieces at the first rumble of such an uprising.

He wrote Sir Henry Clinton, complaining about "the most wanton, unprecedented and inhuman murder that ever disgraced the Arms of a civilized people." He insisted that Captain Lippincott be turned over to him, obviously for hanging purposes.

Clinton had already resigned, and he only hoped to keep out of trouble until his resignation was accepted and his relief had arrived. He replied, politely enough, if stiffly, that he would appoint a court of inquiry. He did this. He also rewrote the arrangement with the Board of Associated Loyalists so that such a thing could never happen again.

Washington was not satisfied. He demanded Lippincott. He wrote to Brigadier General Moses Hazen, who was in charge of the prisoners taken at Yorktown, ordering him

to choose by lot a British captain or lieutenant, to be sent
to the Continental lines in New Jersey, there to be executed.
Until that time, the commander-in-chief stipulated, the victim should be treated with every courtesy.

By this time the British board of inquiry in New York
had decided that Captain Lippincott must face a court-
martial, and this Captain Lippincott was doing. Sir Henry
Clinton had received news that his resignation was accepted,
and he had sailed for home, leaving the British forces in
America in the temporary command of a fat and indecisive
Scot, Major General James Robertson.

It was unthinkable that Robertson would have turned
over Lippincott to the rebels. Nor would Sir Henry Clinton
have done so. Nor would the new commander-in-chief Sir
Guy Carleton, who was on his way to New York. The British
might hang Lippincott *themselves,* if a court-martial found
him guilty, but they would not hand him over to the enemy.
When Washington had offered them André if they would
give back the traitor Benedict Arnold, the British never
hesitated. How could they? Yet they had execrated Arnold
and loved André.

Nobody seemed to have had anything against Captain
Lippincott, whom the court-martial, after as many delays
as they could contrive, found not guilty. Lippincott's orders
had been verbal, not written, and it was never to be brought
out who had issued them; but the British at least were
certain that *he* was not guilty, and they so notified George
Washington.

Washington in his order to Hazen had stipulated that
there be chosen "a British Captain who is an Unconditional
Prisoner, if such a one is in your possession; if not, a Lieutenant under the same circumstances from among the
prisoners at any of the Posts either in Pennsylvania or Maryland." [53] He learned a little later that there probably wasn't

any such person, and he wrote a much shorter letter to Hazen commanding him to pick the victim "from among all the British Captains who are prisoners either under Capitulation or Convention," and to do it right away.

Most of the officers taken at Yorktown had been permitted to return to England, but a few of the juniors were left, and Hazen found that he had thirteen captains under his command at Lancaster, Pennsylvania. Sighing, he summoned them, together with their prisoner-commander, a major, and announced that the drawing would start. There were thirteen slips of paper in one basket, each containing the name of a captain, and thirteen in another basket, all of them blank except for the one on which was written "Unfortunate." A drummer boy would do the drawing, General Hazen said.

The Britishers promptly, and most properly, demurred. They had surrendered, they pointed out, under articles that ensured them against any manner of subsequent punishment. "We refuse to have any share in a business which directly violates the terms of the treaty that placed us within General Washington's power," they declared in writing.

There were fourteen articles in the agreement reached at Yorktown 19 October 1781, and Washington had read and initialed each of them separately before he signed the thing, which was afterward signed by the Comte de Rochambeau for the French Army and the Comte de Barras, representing Admiral de Grasse, who had thought it best to stay with his fleet, for the French Navy.

The last article, No. XIV, read: "No article of capitulation to be infringed on pretence of reprisals; and if there be any doubtful expressions in it, they are to be interpreted according to the common meaning and acceptation of the words."

Thus, the British officers were absolutely right. Never-

theless General Hazen had his orders. The drawing was
held.

Not until the twelfth draw was the name of a captain
matched with the slip that read "Unfortunate." It was that
of Charles Asgill of the First Foot Guards,[54] a Westminster
graduate, at nineteen the youngest of the group. This is the
one who would be hanged. He was locked up.

The major, James Gordon, who had never ceased to
protest, was permitted to go with the lad when he was taken
to Philadelphia as his first step on the way to the grave.
Gordon saw that the honor of France was also involved.
De Grasse, de Barras, and Rochambeau long since had returned to their homeland, so Gordon wrote to the French
ambassador stationed in Philadelphia, the capital of the new
country. He got only a formal and non-committal answer.

Charles Asgill was the son of a baronet, who was pros-
trated with grief. His mother, that lovely lady, and his
adoring young sister, were everywhere wept for. It was
feared that they were losing their reason. The boy—for he
was no more—had become the most important person in the
military life of two continents. Not only were the Americans
involved in his fate, and, understandably, the British too,
but the French as well wrung their hands, wailing. In
France indeed Captain Asgill's had become a *cause célèbre*.
Poems were written about this poor subaltern, whose portrait—based on imagination, since there was no authentic
likeness in existence—was circulated everywhere. "Is he still
alive?" persons disembarking in France from America were
asked by their friends on the shore even before their
health was inquired after; and it was always understood
who was meant.

Washington's headquarters at Newburgh-on-Hudson
was inundated with pleas and protests. He refused to answer
them. Even when Lady Asgill wrote from England he did

not respond. He had announced in advance that he would take this attitude. He must have Captain Lippincott, or Captain Asgill would swing. Of course he would not see Captain Asgill himself, or answer any of the boy's pitiful letters. In the same way General Washington had refused to see Major André when André was under sentence to die as a spy. The commander-in-chief clearly could not trust his own heart.

The very peace talks in Paris were being endangered by the Asgill business; and if the United States did not very soon get peace, a formal, recognizable peace, it would fall apart.

Carleton had arrived in New York, to take over the supreme command. A tactful man, a kindly man, quite different from the stiff Clinton, the hesitant Robertson, or William Howe the hard-drinking gambler, he tried hard to settle the Asgill matter; but he got nowhere. Washington it would seem was not to be moved.

General Cornwallis, an opponent for whom the American commander-in-chief had the highest respect, wrote personally from England, enclosing Lady Asgill's heart-wringing letter. It made no difference.

All sorts of postponements were arranged. The British court-martial that had cleared Captain Lippincott had sat as long as it decently could, and some thought longer. Washington was adamant. Sundry substitutes were suggested, all of them prisoners: Lieutenant Turner of the New Jersey Volunteers; an unnamed man in prison in Winchester, Virginia; a lad lately from Eton, Captain Eyre Coote, and *he* was only *eighteen;* also Captain John Schaack of the 57th Foot, until his capture stationed on Staten Island. There was something against each of these. Charles Asgill remained the one.

He was moved to Chatham, New Jersey, Major Gordon

sticking with him all the while, and writing, writing. Months went by, and any day he could expect to be led forth to the gallows.

Washington the cautious turned the matter over to the Continental Congress, but Congress temporized, dumping it back into his lap. And so it went, while the world waited.

Major Gordon's first idea had been a good one. The French ambasador at Philadelphia, the Chevalier de la Luzerne, had thought it unwise to become directly involved, but he agreed with the major that the honor of France was involved, and he pointed this out in a letter to his superior, the French foreign minister, the Comte de Vergennes, who at about this same time got a personal letter from Lady Asgill.

Vergennes was a dry stick, a man of facts and figures, a man not likely to be stirred by humane emotions. But he could sense the feeling of France; and maybe after all he did have some sort of heart. He wrote to George Washington, enclosing Lady Asgill's letter to him, Vergennes.

Vergennes's own letter was a velvet glove, and whether there was an iron fist inside of it was a problem for the American. After all, without France the new republic would collapse. Washington pointed this out to Congress, to whom he sent the letters, and Congress hastily agreed, authorizing him to do whatever he thought best. This excuse to get out of the case was something Washington had been seeking for a long while. He sat down to write, for the first time, to Captain Asgill.

It was early April when Joshua Huddy was strung up. It was October when Congress told George Washington to go ahead. And it was early November before Charles Asgill, in Chatham, learned that he was free without qualification.

I cannot take leave of you, **Sir,** without assuring

you, that, in whatever light my agency in this un-pleasing affair may be viewed I was never influenced, through the whole of it, by sanguinary motives, but what I conceived a sense of my duty.[55]

The young captain, delighted, took the next ship home, where, rather unexpectedly, after that harrowing experience, he elected to remain in the army, in which he was to become a lieutenant general, a higher rank than ever had been held by the man who sentenced him to death.[56]

The peace talks in Paris were resumed.

14

"To Lie for His Country"

WILL ROGERS USED TO SAY that the United States never lost a war and never won a peace.

He was wrong on the first count; but it must be remembered that he said this before Viet Nam. He was wrong on the second count as well. It had reference, of course, to the curious American belief that foreign diplomats, all done up with their medals and their titles, habitually rode rings around the simple, gawky, homespun American envoys, who knew nothing of such serpentine ways. Today, in this striped-pants era, things might be different, and there could just be a modicum of truth in the all-Europeans-are-Machiavellian notion. However that may be, in the settlement of the first two wars the United States fought—both, as it happened, against Great Britain—the republican envoys made fools of the smooth-spoken European veterans.

The United States had been soundly beaten, again and again, in the War of 1812 (the only American land victory, New Orleans, had not yet taken place when the envoys foregathered at Ghent in August of 1814), yet the shrewd Yankees came out with a triumphant *status quo ante*, which

in effect put everything back to where it had been before
the fighting started. This astonishing result came about
largely because of the weakness of the British delegation.
To England, at the time, the conference at Ghent was a
side-show. The big tent was at Vienna. Napoleon, that
monumental disturber of the peace, had been overthrown
and cast into a cozy exile; he had escaped, had rallied infatuated Frenchmen to himself once again, and at last had
been thoroughly, indisputably beaten at Waterloo. What
the conference in Austria would settle was not merely one
war but a whole series of wars. Nothing like it ever had
happened before. It was to be the World Series, the Oxford-
Cambridge race, of diplomacy; and every Foreign Office
employee above the rank of office boy was pulling every
string in sight for the purpose of getting there, of being
seen there. In consequence, the delegates that the nation
sent to Ghent were a fourth-rate lot: Lord Gambier, a retired naval personage, an earlier Colonel Blimp, famous
chiefly because of his swiftly incarnadined face; Dr. William Adams, a crass, talkative fellow who was supposed to
be an expert in maritime law; and a young man named
Henry Goulburn. In the pit with these were Jonathan Russell, the United States minister to Sweden; Henry Clay, one
of the best poker players in Congress; the Swiss-born financial wizard, Albert Gallatin; and that erudite sourpuss John
Quincy Adams. There was, really, no contest. The Britishers
were lucky that they were permitted to go home with their
shirts on.

No such diversion had existed when the Treaty of Paris
of 1782 ended the American Revolution. The British there
were obliged not only to settle an eight-year struggle with
the American colonies, states now, but also to bring to an
end the wars with the American allies, France, Spain, and
even the Netherlands. Everything hung, however, on the
United States; it must come first; and the British, in con-

sequence, fielded one of their strongest diplomatic teams. This was met by some of the smartest horse-traders in the business.

Opposites, the glum, disapproving John Adams, the gay Ben Franklin, started the proceedings for the United States, as they were to finish them. Dr. Franklin, for all his years a wag of the first water—he was in his upper seventies as the peace conference got under way—had learned the fine art of frivolity, which endeared him to his hosts, the French. He performed wonders while seeming only to be telling a funny story. "The old conjurer," John Adams grudgingly called him; and despite the differences in their personalities, their temperaments, their ages, they got along beautifully. Adams supplying the vinegar, Franklin the oil, they mixed a savory salad dressing, these diplomatic chefs.

There came along, early in the proceedings, from Spain, where he had endured an exquisite snubbing as ambassador, John Jay, a New York lawyer of Huguenot descent, a man dry and stubborn, slabsided, sententious. He seldom got excited, only when the subject was religion, for he hated the Roman Catholic Church. He was an extremely able, if uncompanionable, envoy. He was particularly welcome to old-line Patriots like Adams and Franklin because for so long, during the independence-emerging period, he had seemed to waver toward Loyalism. For a long time he had held out for a compromise with the Crown. With John Dickinson he had co-drafted the so-called Olive Branch Petition, the Continental Congress's last appeal to the King; but when this was ignored, and he was obliged at last to take sides, he plumped for the Patriot cause. He was a tower of strength at Paris.

When Lord Germain brought the news of Yorktown to Lord North the latter had staggered as though hit in the chest by a musket ball (as Germain in fact had been, at Fontenoy), crying "Oh, God! it is all over!" This was the attitude of most Englishmen. In fact, though there were to be no more battles, a state of war still existed, a condition of affairs that could not be concluded until the men in Paris had completed their task. The siege of New York, if it could be called that, went on. Royal Navy vessels snapped up American prizes on the high seas, the narrow seas as well. But there was almost no shooting anymore. This was why the killing of young John Laurens came as such a shock to American Patriots, and especially to the members of the peace commission in Paris, who were expecting to be joined by his father, Henry Laurens, any day now.

John Laurens, a South Carolinian, had been educated in England and in Switzerland, and had read for the law. The scion of a wealthy family, he had never wavered in his devotion to the Patriot cause. He had fought on the Brandy-wine and at Germantown and Monmouth, and he had winged General Charles Lee in a duel because he believed that Lee had belittled the commander-in-chief George Washington. Young Laurens was one of Washington's best aides and could serve as an interpreter, for he was fluent in French and knew some German as well. Back in his home state he had fought at Charleston against Prevost, then had gone to Georgia to help defend Savannah, his rank by this time being that of Lieutenant Colonel. At Guilford Court House he had served as a brigadier general in the Virginia militia. He had been wounded at Coosa-hatchie Pass, captured when Charleston fell, and exchanged. He had helped gallantly in the storming of a British outpost before Yorktown, the last open fight of the war. Then he had returned to South Carolina to supervise the restoration of his father's estates, where, at Combahee Ferry, 27 August 1782, he had been shot by a trigger-happy redcoat, member of a foraging squad he was trying to drive away.

John Laurens was not yet thirty when he died. The

killing was legitimate; that is, it was allowable under the laws of war, so that nobody was court-martialed. It is generally written down as the last fatality of the American Revolution, though there may have been other, less legal slaughterings along the frontier, where murder was a commonplace.

In the circumstances the peace commissioners at Paris did not really expect the father, Henry Laurens, former president of the Continental Congress, to join them. He did so, though he was late, arriving on the scene Friday, 29 November, after most of the really hard work had been done.

The fifth peace commissioner, Thomas Jefferson, never did show up in Paris. His reason for staying away has not survived. He had been the second governor of the state of Virginia—Patrick Henry was the first—but his term of office was over, and he was, for him, idle.

Virginians were sharp in their criticism of the Great Penman's absence. They complained that they had not been properly represented at the conference.

Until the time of the Revolution, American merchants had operated under a heads-you-win-tails-I-lose system of exchange. They bought from England more than they could possibly sell her, and in spite of some side profit, unrecorded, from smuggling, they were going deeper and deeper into debt, seemingly all unaware that this was a trend that could not go on forever, since sooner or later the English dealers would want to be paid.[57] Interest increased the obligation, even after the war had halted commerce between the two countries, so that by 1791 the various American states owed £4,930,650 to British merchants; and about half of this was owed by Virginia.[58] That state was so fiscally unhappy that at the end of the war she had gone back upon tobacco as a currency, there being no cash; but the weed was selling as low as 18 shillings a hundredweight, while Negroes, the state's other great commodity, were going at anywhere from £20 to £30 apiece for prime males, a ruinous price.[59]

It was the Negroes, the slaves, that formed the basis of Virginia's chief complaint. The colony and later the state was the principal "breeding shed" of America, a position of which she was not proud, though she took full advantage of it. Nowhere else did blacks multiply so well in captivity. At the outbreak of the Revolution there were about five hundred thousand slaves in the American mainland colonies, and of these about one hundred thousand were to be found in South Carolina, seventy thousand to eighty thousand each in Maryland and North Carolina, twenty-five thousand in New York, ten thousand in New Jersey, six thousand each in Pennsylvania and Connecticut, five thousand in Massachusetts, and about four thousand in Rhode Island. Georgia, which was growing rapidly, had more than ten thousand. In Virginia there were at least two hundred thousand.

Rampaging redcoats, once the war had been diverted from the north to the south, in 1780, seized upon slaves right and left as legitimate spoils of war, comparable to stored tobacco, indigo, rice, or any other kind of rebel-owned goods. In the Carolinas such seizures were not treasury-shaking, since so many of the landowners in those colonies were certified Loyalists whose property, human or otherwise, was of course untouchable; but in Virginia, virtually 100 percent Patriotic, the British had taken, according to Jefferson's own estimate, some thirty thousand Negroes. They did not *free* these men! They sold them to planters in the British West Indies, where the poor devils would have a much worse time of it than ever they had had in Virginia. And now Virginia was demanding £500,000 indemnity. She wouldn't accept any peace settlement, she declared, that did not include this. The British flatly refused.

Virginians wailed that the Wise Men of the East through their peace conference representative John Adams were getting more than their share of attention when they clamored for a continuation of their Grand Banks fishing rights, while nobody was doing anything about that £500,-000 claim for whisked-away slaves.

Adams did work hard for the Grand Banks project. His "right" to fish there was whittled down to a "liberty" to do so, a fact that he regretted, for like the good lawyer that he was he looked forward to a time when conceivably the "liberty" might be infringed, whereas the "right" never could have been; but it was a victory all the same.

Franklin, the first in the field, without any sort of fuss started the dickering with a bland demand that all of Canada be turned over to the new republic. It is certain that he never dreamed of *getting* Canada, for which he had not the shadow of a claim; but the demand remained, a *quid pro quo*, something to be swapped for something else when the time came. To this Adams added, almost as though by afterthought, Nova Scotia.

Franklin also threatened to demand restitution for the burning of sundry American towns—Charlestown, Massachusetts, which the Royal Navy set afire in order to clear the way for an assault upon Bunker Hill; Falmouth, Maine; [60] Norfolk, Virginia; New London and Fairfield, Connecticut; and Esopus, New York.[61] He never had a chance of collecting such indemnity, and indeed he never did make a formal demand for it; but the threat was useful as a weapon in reserve.

The Americans all the while serenely accepted full independence as an assumed, non-arguable point. So, they pointed out, did France, which would not even begin to talk about peace otherwise, not to mention Spain and Holland. The British tried in vain to get some qualification here.

There was an influenza epidemic sweeping northern Europe at this time—John Jay was laid up for several weeks in the very middle of the negotiations—and one of its victims was the Marquis of Rockingham, who died in London, causing Horace Walpole to remark that now the Crown devolved upon the King of England. *That* personage simply could not think of permitting his American colonies to float away, and he was a prodigiously stubborn man.[62] North had resigned, perforce, and had been succeeded by Lord Shelbourne, who was personally opposed to independence for America, and who was getting letters threatening him with assassination if he conceded such independence.

There was a sense of urgency about the negotiations in Paris that both sides deplored, but it was especially remarkable among the British. The new republic teetered on the verge of bankruptcy, while its unpaid army was kept from dissolution only by the continued presence in camp of George Washington, who, poor man, was aching to get back to Mount Vernon. In England the political situation was much worse. Peace was absolutely imperative, and it must be made soon; yet France would not even begin to discuss terms until the Americans had been satisfied; for France, despite all of those dire predictions about her infidelity, was proving a good friend, a firm friend.

The negotiators in Paris, too, had to take into consideration events elsewhere in the world. That September a badly mismanaged Franco-Spanish attack upon Gibraltar was repulsed, strengthening the British hand, as had Rodney's defeat of the French fleet in the West Indies April 12. Nevertheless, the English were desperate, and the Americans knew this and took advantage of it.

As was the custom of the time, large chunks of the New World were dangled like bright bait before parties in dispute, the West Indian islands in particular being passed around like biscuits at a tea table. Thus, Spain badly though she wanted Gibraltar back, refused to trade West Florida and the Gulf Coast, the "waterfront" of the decaying Spanish empire, for it; while France at one time or other was asked for Dominica, Guadeloupe, the Bahamas, Trinidad, and Minorca, St. Lucia also being mentioned, and even, briefly, Martinique. The Americans at Paris did not participate in these almost-deals, but they had to take them into consideration.

The overriding issue, all through the proceedings, the one thing upon which all the others hung, was the question of what should be done about the Loyalists. This almost wrecked the conference.

The British insisted that before they could even talk about independence they must have some assurance that the breaking-away colonies would reimburse the Loyalists, who had lost their land, their homes, their professions or businesses. This must come first. So?

The Americans would reply that they had no authority to treat of this subject. Congress had not included it in their instructions.

More than two years before this time Horace Walpole had written to a friend [63] that there was "as little chance of recovering America as of reconquering the Holy Land." It may be that the British delegates had never heard this. More likely they clung to the no-independence threat in the wild hope that it could be made to frighten the American delegates. This it never did do. The Americans simply shook their heads when the subject of restitution was broached.

Again and again the British would open a session with this demand, and again and again the Americans would lift their shoulders to their ears.

The conference was being held, for all practical purposes, on the enemy's ground. From Paris to London and back again, by fast messenger, would take a week, provided that the Channel was not in an unamiable mood and provided also that the desired minister or secretary did not happen to be vacationing out of town. From Paris to Philadelphia and back took anywhere from five to nine months. If this had seemed for a little while a handicap to the Americans, they soon twisted it into an advantage. Cornered, as they so often were, with another demand for some show of recompense for the Loyalists, exiled and still at home, the Americans would shrug yet again, and spread their palms, and ask, "Should we send home for further instructions? Do you want that?"

In the treaty as finally agreed upon Congress was urged by the delegates to recommend "earnestly" to the several states that they make some manner of restitution to the Loyalists. None of them ever did.

For the rest, the treaty gave America virtually everything for which she had asked, and more besides. Benjamin Franklin had graciously dropped his demand for the whole of Canada, and the United States was acknowledged to be a free and sovereign nation that extended west as far as the Mississippi River.

Shelbourne had been ousted, and Lord North was back in power, his foreign minister being Charles James Fox ("Boreas and Reynard" Mr. Burke liked to call them), and these two pushed it through somehow, regretfully, shamefacedly.

The signing took place in Paris Saturday, 30 November, 1782. This was St. Andrew's Day, which the British delegates professed to take as a good sign, for two of the three of them, and the secretary of the delegation as well, were Scottish. In fact it was a thumping big American victory.

15

A Tragedy of Errors

THE QUESTION REMAINED, when all else had been settled in Paris, in London, and even in Charleston and New York: What should be done with the Loyalists? They were, themselves, apprehensive. In several of the "small surrenders" they believed that they had been sold out by a home country that found them inconvenient, a belief japing Patriots encouraged. They would quote:

'Tis an honor to serve the bravest of nations,
And be left to be hanged in their capitulations.

This was unfair. The ministers of the crown, to give them credit, were doing everything possible to make things easy for such Loyalists as had already gone abroad as well as for those who remained in what had become the United States; but the problem was a knotty one, for the Loyalists were querulous, edgy, acerb, while the Patriots were in no forgiving mood.

The refusal of the new states to do anything for the dispossessed losers shocked and surprised the English ministers of state, who so ardently believed that they *should*. The Loyalists, both at home and in exile, until the very end never had doubted that the British arms would triumph, restoring the authority of the King in America. Yorktown had come as a terrible shock to them; but when at last they had come to believe it, they demanded, snarling, to be told what the government was going to do for them. Closer than the English to those who had won, they knew how hard the hatred would die, if indeed it ever did, and the vindictiveness that the Patriots were displaying was exactly what their late enemies would have predicted; but the men in London, the men who managed imperial affairs, were jolted.

Sighing, Whitehall appointed its own commission of compensation, which took many years to do the job, and at one time had three authorized agents in America.

The commission went over each plea and petition carefully, ignoring the wails raised by necessitous exiles. It refused to allow compensation for uncultivated lands, for rents, for estates purchased after the war, for incomes of offices received during the war—Joseph Galloway, for example, had been paid £300 a year as police magistrate and another £770 as superintendent of the port as long as Philadelphia was occupied—for anticipated professional profits, or losses in trade or labor or by the British Army, or losses through depreciated paper money or captures at sea. There were many claims left, even so. Two thousand and sixty-three persons had entered claims by the last day for filing, 26 March 1784, and these totaled £7,046,278, plus debts amounting to £2,354,135.

Counting the claims on the other side of the sea, there was a total of 5,072, though 954 of these were withdrawn or disallowed. The remaining 4,118—1,401 of them in

Canada—asked for more than £8,000,000 and in time were paid slightly in excess of £3,000,000.

The whole business, it was estimated,[64] could have cost the British government as much as $30,000,000, and this was in addition to land grants, pensions, and annuities, *plus* the cost of administering the commission itself.

Slightly over one-third of the claims were allowed: the board's final report showed that the claims had totaled £8,026,045, and of this £3,292,452 had been allowed.

Three hundred and three exiles were pensioned for life, though only eighteen of these got more than £200 a year. Galloway got £500, almost as much as Robert Eden, the last royal governor of Maryland, who happened to be a brother of the undersecretary of state. William Franklin got £800 a year.

Some of the doughtiest fighters among the Loyalists were scamped. Colonel David Fanning, the South Carolina hero, a Tory leader who had been sensationally successful in the field, did not do as well with the compensation commissioners as he had done against the Patriots. He put in a claim for £1,635, and got £60.

Some of the large landowners did very well. The famous Indian agent, Sir John Johnson, was granted £103,-162. Oliver De Lancey got £108,957, the largest single award. Gentleman Johnny Burgoyne, in striving to explain his surrender, had charged his chief civilian advisor Philip Skene with having arranged to have a military road built through his property, a road that could have been better placed elsewhere, and said that this might have helped to cause the disaster. Nevertheless Skene listed among his losses 56,350 acres, a barn, a stable, 950 cords of firewood, 2,000 sawlogs, 8,000 pipe staves, eight Negroes, and twenty cows, and he was awarded £22,000.

Once it had become too late to matter, once the conflict had been decided, the truth emerged that in all of this war, this tragedy of errors, the greatest mistake was that made by the British military authorities when they spurned the use of local volunteers, Loyalists, despised as amateur soldiers.

The King's men in the colonies could not be reproached for failing to do whatever lay within their power to put down this, to them, unnatural rebellion. They had been poorly organized, poorly informed, badly led—when they could be said to be led at all—but from the very beginning they had been willing and even eager to fight. They had tried to enlist in the prestigious British army. These efforts, starting in Boston at the time of the siege, for a long time either had been pushed aside or had been accepted in a patronizing spirit, as who would say "Well, if we get 'em into uniform at least we'll keep 'em out of mischief." The British were to feel a manpower pinch, and to have resorted to the expensive and unpopular system of hiring German mercenaries, before the old prejudice against Americans as fighting men could be overcome sufficiently to allow them to let the colonists show what they could do in the field.

The Loyalists never were flaunted for propaganda purposes, as they might well have been; and because they took royalist-sounding names for the regiments they formed, and because many of them wore the standard red uniform, they were not always recognized by those just behind them in history *as* Loyalists, *as* Americans. In fact, without any drum rolls or the flip-flapping of gilt-edged flags, they did a good job.

The American colonies, when war started, contained perhaps seven hundred thousand men of fighting age, but nothing like this number ever served in any military capacity whatever, and those who did serve, in the Continental Army at least, came and went with such bewildering rapidity that General Washington never could depend upon them. In 1776 the Continental Army and the various militias all put together—and they never *were* put together—held only about one-eighth of the potential fighting force. By 1779/80 this proportion had dropped to one-sixteenth and it was still falling; for the Patriots, it seemed then, were losing interest in their cause.

Between thirty thousand and fifty thousand Loyalists fought for the King in the American Revolution, in the regular British army alone; and there were many thousands more serving in the militia and the various guerrilla groups. At the end of the war there were eight thousand American Loyalists *in uniform in the British army.* Washington at that same time had barely nine thousand under arms, and his desertions were increasing.

There is every reason to believe that the Loyalist side was growing stronger every day at the time when the British tossed a towel into the ring. If the British had accepted this conflict for what it was, a civil war, and if they had furnished their American well-wishers with leadership and supplies, both of which they badly needed, the war, even after Yorktown, might have gone their way; for France had done all that she could be expected to do, and the Patriots left in uniform were tired, and hungry, and clamoring for their pay, so that they could not have held out much longer. But the British attitude was: if our boys can't do it it can't be done. Here they were inflexible.

The capture of Charleston, South Carolina, late in the war, was the greatest single victory for either side; and in this memorable action there were as many American Loyalists as British regulars, as many as there were Hessians.

King's Mountain [65] was, after Bunker Hill, the fiercest fight of the war. *Everybody on both sides,* excepting only

Battle of King's Mountain

the British commanding officer, Lieutenant Colonel Patrick Ferguson, a Scot, was American. Ferguson was killed in the battle. Nine of the losers, that is the Loyalists, were hanged out-of-hand at the edge of the field afterward, having been denounced as traitors. Most of the Loyalists who engaged in this meeting were from New York, and the second-in-command on their side was a New Yorker, a De Peyster; but the hanged men all were from the South, where the war lately had taken a personal turn.

What to do with these enlisted personnel at the end of the war was a problem. A few at the news of Yorktown deserted to the enemy lines and joined the Continental Army just before the formal truce. A few elected to stay in the British army, notoriously no bed of roses, and were welcomed there. Most of them stuck together as units, and were mustered out in places held still by the British, chiefly New York City, and these, as civilians, were treated like the other proven Loyalists—that is, they were given small grants of land and shipped off by land or by water to Canada, that vast, sprawling, sparsely populated territory to the north. The trip could be perilous. In November of 1783 the transport *Martha*, from Maryland, sank off Seal Island in the Bay of Fundy, and 250 persons were drowned, all of them Loyalists. But—others got through.

You Can't Go Home Again

Whilst hostilities lasted there were all sorts of plans for sheltering the Loyalists. These men and women had been stigmatized as "objects of resentment of the public" or "enemies of the liberties of America" or sometimes simply as "incorrigible," and it had been stipulated:

> That Tories, with their brats and wives,
> Should fly to save their wretched lives.

The wording didn't matter, for it all came to the same thing. Those who were known couldn't stay home. There must have been some—but not many—who lasted the war out by keeping their mouths determinedly shut, never speaking up for King and Parliament or permitting their feelings to show in any way, who might pray for George III some nights in the secrecy of their several bedchambers but were clams in public. When they became known, their presence intolerable in the opinion of their neighbors, they might be shipped in guarded groups to some other colony or state, which was politely asked to take care of them, though it is hard to see how this could solve the problem, for their new jailors simply moved them along. These prisoners as they passed through small towns were sometimes stoned by civilians; but they were not otherwise mistreated. They were not clapped into concentration camps, and their temporary keepers were not cruel to them. There was never any scandal attached to these brief imprisonments, not like the British army's prison hulks in New York harbor, for instance, where turnkeys notoriously "fed the dead and starved the living."

Still another method of getting rid of Loyalists while the war was on was that of shoving them off into the grim western reaches of the colonies, and particularly of the southern colonies, where they could melt into the frontier, a place where questions were not asked. Some went farther, voluntarily. Some trekked up the Mohawk trail, or filtered through the Cumberland Gap in order to settle along the Ohio Valley or even on the banks of the Mississippi. The first westward push of Anglo-Saxon settlers into those parts was made up very largely of supporters of the King, who were not challenging the wilderness from any spirit of derring-do but simply because they had been pushed.

Most of the wartime scheme for transportation of the Loyalists, however, were temporary expedients. Like the enclaves proposed for Maryland and for Maine they were based on the assumption that the royal arms soon would prevail and order would be restored in America. They were stopgaps, nothing more. Any that might even hint of a permanent answer to the problem was tut-tutted as trivial. For instance, there was one proposal that the Loyalists be shipped to Germany to take the places of those "Hessians" from Hesse-Cassel, Hesse-Hanau, Brunswick, Anspach-Bay-reuth, Waldeck, and Anhalt-Zerbst who might never return from their American assignment.[66] Nothing was done about this, nor yet about the even wilder scheme to ship all American Loyalists to the other side of the world where Captain Cook recently had discovered a new continent, Australia.

Eight of the thirteen new states specifically banished listed Loyalists, and the other five virtually did. Omitting those who had slipped past the frontier and become lost in the vast reaches of what was soon to be known as the Middle West—for their migrations were haphazard and their settlements seldom formally recorded—those who quit the new nation as political exiles fell into three classes:

There were those who went to England, those who went to the West Indies or Florida, those who went to Canada.

> The Germans live in Germany;
> Italians live in Rome;
> The French they live in Gay Paree;
> But the English live at Home.

The ditty had not yet been written, but it could be applied to the first Loyalist exiles, the ones who went to England, their hearts full of hope, the earliest away, the richest, in time the most unhappy. Some few of these already had been in England when the war clouds started to spread, studying art there perhaps, or reading for the bar, or taking holy orders, and they remained there, waiting for the situation in America to right itself. These could not properly be dubbed exiles. The others were fervent Tories, hailing in general from the northern colonies, and all their lives they had thought of themselves as English, as they had thought of England as Home, spelled, even in their minds, with that capital H. They were to be disillusioned.

It could be that some of them expected to be greeted

as heroes. They were not. In the first place, they learned to their chagrin that large numbers of native Englishmen openly favored the colonial cause, speaking for it, arguing in its behalf, some of them even collecting money to aid the rebels, which seemed to the newly arrived visitors little short of sacrilege. Others did extend sympathy to them for a little while—after all, they had *tried* to do the right thing, eh?—but these men in time began to wonder if the visitors after all were not quitters, leaving the field even before the fight began; and some too looked down upon them as poor relations.

There were many complaints. The plumbing did seem the equal to that of New England, and the newspapers were almost as good, once you got used to them; but the fireplaces were tiny, stingy apertures, and the food of course was unspeakable, everything boiled. Worst of all was the attitude of the average Englishman toward these refugees when he learned that most of them were tradesmen. It was the custom of the time for the English to turn up their noses at "those in trade," something that the exiles simply could not understand. In America the most respected persons, the most respectable families—the Peabodys, the Stuyvesants, the Rensselaers, and De Lanceys, and Laurenses, and Wentworths—were trading people. This made them unacceptable? Samuel Curwen, as dignified and distinguished a visitor as it would be possible to conceive, had given his occupation as "merchant," and for a long time he wondered why his hosts passed him by, brushed him aside; until one day, quite by chance, he happened to mention that he had also, in the colonies, been an admiralty court judge, and then suddenly they were all bowing to him in the park, while invitations poured in, for a judge is a gentleman. Americans learned to accept this attitude, but never to like it.

London was noisy, smelly, and appallingly expensive,

and the Americans too were shocked by the Gomorrhean goings-on there; yet London was the seat of government and the place they must go to in order to seek relief. They abominated it. They huddled together in their own favorite coffeehouses, establishments spurned by the "real" English, where they told one another how sorry for one another they were, wondering when their fellow countrymen would come to their senses and sue for peace and for the restoration of the old order. Only those who had assured if small incomes could go to nearby towns to live: Pimlico was a favorite. Some went all the way to the north of England, and Thomas Flucker, a Tory of Tories, father-in-law of Henry Knox, went to Wales. One and all, they would have agreed with their most distinguished member, Thomas Hutchinson, the last royal governor of Massachusetts, who avowed that he would "rather die in a little country farmhouse in New England than in the best nobleman's seat" at Home.

East and West Florida (the latter consisting of what is now the Florida panhandle as well as the southern halves of Alabama and Mississippi) had been tossed back and forth between England and Spain so often that they could not be regarded as a safe refuge. They were presently Spanish; and the Loyalists who had fled there found it impossible to wrest a living out of that bare, flat, sunburnt land, so that most of them moved to the British West Indian colonies of Jamaica and the Bahamas, though a few went to Bermuda. These people originally had come from Charleston, South Carolina, or that vicinity, and the ones who had left before the final departure of the redcoats were permitted to take their slaves with them, so that they prospered on the land granted them by the government. There was a much larger movement of continental Loyalists to the West Indies directly from South Carolina, especially after the war had ended. More went to Jamaica than to the Bahamas, but Jamaica was a busy crowded place, where they were more or less lost, while in the thinly populated Bahamas they could make their mark. Colonel Andrew Deveaux, who conducted the last military action of the war, recapturing Nassau (Spain had recently joined France in war against Great Britain) with a mere handful of men, all of whom were rewarded with land grants, came from Charleston. So did John Wells, who in August of 1784 established the first newspaper in that part of the world, the *Bahama Gazette*. These exiles in general favored New Providence and Great Abaco, though they were scattered over many more islands of the group, and there are residents of the Bahamas to this day who boast of their descent from them.

Canada was the catchall. That was where most of the outgoers went, come-willy-come-nilly. Despite the long land border, most went by sea. Benedict Arnold had led a daring expedition through the Maine woods and into Quebec early in the war; but Benedict Arnold was a genius; and to the average fleeing Loyalist, even if it happened that he was unencumbered with household goods and supplies, that forest was and always would be impenetrable. The Lake George–Lake Champlain–Richelieu River route since the defeat of Gentleman Johnny Burgoyne at Saratoga was firmly in the hands of Continental troops, who could be counted upon at least to strip of all their belongings any Loyalists they happened to intercept. The upper St. Lawrence country and the gateway to Canada provided by the Niagara region between Lakes Ontario and Erie offered a flat approach through western New York State, but it was an approach overrun by the dreaded Iroquois, who even after the war might jump this way or might jump that, and whose scalp-taking proclivities and fondness for slow fires were well known.

Some few fugitives, in straggling parties, did take the land route, settling eventually in the St. Lawrence Valley, most of them at or near Sorel or Three Rivers, but the majority went by sea. There were four big movements of Loyalists out of the country. There was the original exodus from Boston after Washington, by fortifying Dorchester Heights, had made that city uninhabitable by General Howe and his redcoats. This, a brilliantly executed retreat that marked the end of the seige of Boston, consisted of 170 vessels, in which Howe's own military forces, about 14,500 men, were joined by more than 1,100 Loyalists and 667 camp followers. It sailed 17 March, 1776, which was not being celebrated as St. Patrick's Day, for there were very few Irishmen in Boston then. There was a large movement of Pennsylvania and Maryland Loyalists from Philadelphia just before Clinton evacuated that capital in 1778, and a similar though somewhat smaller one from Newport, Rhode Island, the following year, when the British had decided to give up *that* port. New York City had been the British military headquarters in America ever since it was taken by Howe's forces in the "battle" of Manhattan, 15 September 1776, and it was also a favorite gathering place for Loyalists from upper New York State and from nearby colonies, who made it their home, perforce, during most of the war. After the peace had been signed in Paris it was estimated that a little over 12,000 Loyalists left New York City, Long Island, and Staten Island. A handful went to the Bahamas; but the bulk of them went to Canada—by sea, of course.

Canada at that time was divided into two parts. The Maritime Provinces, so-called, consisted of Nova Scotia, New Brunswick (until 1784 a part of Nova Scotia), and Cape Breton, Prince Edward, and assorted smaller islands. Canada proper was all the rest, most of it a frozen wasteland. This in turn was split into Lower Canada, or Quebec, and Upper Canada. Only the extreme eastern part of Upper Canada, the present Ontario, contained any white settlers.

There might have been a total of a hundred thousand

Loyalist exiles—of whom about thirty-five thousand were
from New York—and at least half of these settled in Canada,
something like thirty-five thousand in the Maritime Provinces, perhaps ten thousand in Quebec, the rest in Ontario.
The popular story has it—and had it, even then—that these
were of a superior breed, largely Harvard graduates, who
enriched the land to which they had been moved. It is
true that some were notable men, men of distinction, who
would have proved a credit to any community. Nova Scotia's
first Supreme Court justices *were* Harvard men, and the first
provincial secretary was an Episcopal minister from New
Jersey. But most of them were artisans or farmers, especially
farmers.

They had an uncomfortable time of it in that place of
fog, of wet, cold, spongy moss, of hardwood trees that resisted clearance—oak, elm, hickory, ash—a place where the
sun seldom shone and where winter seemed to last forever.
Elaborate preparations for their transportation and settlement had been made, but made in London, for the most part,
and London was three thousand miles away. Inevitably
there were shortages and misunderstandings, foul-ups caused
by red tape. Some of the settlers had to spend the first terrible winter in tents, and they were loud in their grumblings.
"Nova Scarcity," the Patriots back home sneered.

Granted, the coast of Nova Scotia was even sterner and
more rockbound, colder too, than that upon which the *Mayflower* passengers had landed, but these latter-day Pilgrims
were much better equipped than those of Plymouth. The
government in England had not only allotted land to them—
five hundred acres a family or three hundred acres for a
single man, all free of quitrent for ten years, plus two
thousand acres per town for each church and one thousand
acres for the erection and maintenance of schools—but it
also provided picks and shovels, axes, fishnets, muskets. It

provided, too, food. Here was the cause of the most cacoph-
onous complaints. The Americans had been accustomed to
good eating, but in Canada, and especially in the Maritime
Provinces, they had to subsist, in some cases for as long as
three years at a stretch, on provisions handed out by the
British navy, which under the grafting ministrations of John
Montagu, the nobleman after whom the sandwich was
named, was at this time in a state of almost unbelievable
rottenness. The food that the shivering outcasts were given
was worm-eaten hardtack and salt pork, salt beef, salt fish,
all very old, most of it malodorous. Yet they survived. They
were not happy, but there was never any widespread suffering. They survived; and their descendants are proud of
them. In Canada alone did the Loyalists of the American
Revolution keep and even glory in their identity. They held
conventions, after a while, and they passed resolutions. They
called themselves the United Empire Loyalists, proudly add-
ing "U.E.L." or simply "U.E." after their signatures, as
thousands still do.

They knew that they could never go back. The heritage
of hatred, at home, was amazing. It seemed to have occurred
to nobody in the new nation to say, "Well, they backed the
wrong horse, so let's forget about it." They were renegades,
and retribution must be theirs. There was to be no forgiveness.

The exceptions were few. Philip Barton Key, a Loyalist,
uncle to the "Star-Spangled Banner" man, after the war was
elected to the Maryland legislature, and in 1806 was even
elected to the federal Congress. Samuel Corwin, the judge-
gentleman, was at long last permitted to return to Salem,
Massachusetts, where he was to die; but he never held
office again.

On the other hand, James K. Polk, when he was campaigning for the Presidency *in 1884,* had to apologize for

his grandfather, Ezekial Polk, who had been a Loyalist at the time of the Revolution.

The sleep of Rip Van Winkle was a unique experience, but his return to his village was marked by a characteristic clamor. His eyesight was failing when he came down the mountain, his beard was white and long, and he found a crowd before the village inn. The sign that swung there did not seem to be the red-coated King George that Rip had known for so many years but rather a man in a *blue* coat, under the portrait of whom was lettered something like "George Washington." When the crowd demanded to know who he was and what he was doing there he quavered, "I am a poor quiet man, a native of this place, and a loyal subject of the King, God bless him!"

"Here a general shout burst from the by-standers—'A tory! a tory! a spy! a refugee! hustle him! away with him!'"

Rip Van Winkle was able to explain himself, and some old-timers identified him and vouched for him, so he was permitted to stay home. He was lucky.

Notes

1. He finished the Revolution as a major general and became the nation's first Secretary of War.

2. *History of England in the Eighteenth Century*, IV, p. 224.

3. Nelson, *The American Tory*, p. 91.

4. Brown, *The King's Friends*, p. 226.

5. "In the assembly of Massachusetts no other member could rival him in minute knowledge of the rules and business of the house, in laborious devotion to its work, in steadiness, endurance, tact, shrewdness, persuasiveness, and in the not very noble art of manipulating committees and caucuses; and while some other men—notably James Otis and John Adams—were far more brilliant in debate, not even their dashing and dazzling speeches could win votes as did the brief, unadorned, informing, and convincing talks of Samuel Adams." Tyler, *The Literary History of the American Revolution*, I, p. 5.

6. Authorities differ as to the origin of the name, but most believe that it first was the Caulkers' Club. This is Webster's preference. The Oxford points out that private clubs at that time, and in particular political clubs, were fond of using Indian names—Tammany, for instance, had been a Delaware sachem—and that *caucausu* (Captain John Smith, always a sloppy speller, in his *Virginia* has it *cawcawaassough*) meant in Algonquin one who urges or advises. Mencken (*American Language*, 4th edition, pp. 107–8) mentions this with approval but does not take sides. Neither

do the compilers of the Smith-Zurcher *Dictionary of American Politics*. The *Dictionary of American English* lists a Boston newspaper quotation referring to a political meeting to be held in West Corcus in 1745, a possibility. The Matthew *Dictionary of Americanisms* speaks well of the theory that the word referred to the conviviality of those early political gatherings and comes from the late Greek *kavkos,* a cup, a theory that the *Encyclopaedia Britannica* dismisses as "farfetched." The latest lexicographer in this field, William Safire (*The New Language of Politics,* Collier Books, New York, 1972), defines the word but does not suggest any derivation. For many years the word "caucus" was thought of as distinctively American, but in our own time the British have taken it up. They use it, however, only in its shaded meaning of advanced political manipulation, skulduggery, and they have coined "caucusing" and "caucusdom," the latter monstrosity unknown in the States.

7. Hosmer, p. 324. "Samuel Adams was, indeed, a man of letters, but he was so only because he was above all things a man of affairs. Of literary art, in certain forms, he was no mean master: of literary art for art's sake, he was entirely regardless. He was perhaps the most voluminous political writer of his time in America, and the most influential political writer of his time in New England; but everything that he wrote was meant for a definite practical purpose, and nothing that he wrote seemed to have had any interest for him aside from that purpose." Tyler, *Literary History*, I, p. 2.

8. These were collected by friends the next morning, and dried, and given back to the lieutenant governor, who later, in England, was to use them in the preparation of volumes II and III of his *History*, a standard work to this day. The entire manuscript, including all the rained-upon pages, now is in the custody of the Division of Archives,

Department of the Massachusetts Secretary of State, State House, Boston.

9. The King had a veto over all acts of legislation passed in most of the colonies, no matter what the colonial form of government, but this was seldom exercised—something less than 5 percent of the time, it has been estimated —and the custom was, once the governor had signed the bill, to go ahead on the assumption that it was already a law.

10. "Underneath all the phenomena of Pilgrim zeal and suffering, more enduring than the Pilgrims' noble compact, unnoticed like the upholding power of earth, lies the primordial fact of the local settlement of the Pilgrims in a form of civic community older than Saxon England, older than the primitive church, and older than the classic states of antiquity. That form of civil community was based upon land." R. G. Adams, *Political Ideas of the American Revolution,* p. 24.

11. Barre, Vermont, the granite center, was named after him, as was Barre, Massachusetts, and, in part, Wilkes-Barre, Pennsylvania. Diacritical marks of any sort are distasteful to Americans, and the acute accent over the "e" has been dropped in each of these places, with the result that out-of-towners, to the annoyance of the natives, tend to pronounce the word "bar."

12. Frothingham, *Rise of the Republic,* pp. 175n–176n.

13. "He [Lord Chatham] mentioned an opinion prevailing here: that America aimed at setting up for itself as an *independent State;* or, at least, to get rid of the *Navigation Acts.* I assured him that, having more than once travelled almost from one end of the continent to the other, and kept a great variety of company, eating, drinking, and conversing with them freely, I never had heard in any conversation from any person, drunk or sober, the least expression of a wish for separation, or hint that such a thing would

be advantageous to America." Benjamin Franklin to his son, William Franklin, 22 March 1775. *Works,* Bigelow edition, V, pp. 445–46.

14. Rudé, *The Crowd in History,* p. 59.

15. ". . . one Warren, a rascally patriot and apothecary of this town, has had the lead in the Provincial Congress." Hulton, *Letters of a Loyalist Lady,* pp. 90–100.

16. Frothingham, *Rise of the Republic,* p. 149.

17. "The important thing about the American Revolution, which the conservative mind overlooked, was not that Parliament was more stupid than tyrannical, not that the English yeoman was less free than the American farmer, but that American farmers and merchants and clergymen and land speculators and shopkeepers and artisans believed with an ardent and consuming belief that their freedom was threatened." Boyd, *Anglo-American Union,* p. 5.

18. *Pennsylvania Magazine of History and Biography,* XXVI, 1902.

19. *Pennsylvania Magazine of History,* XXI, p. 484.

20. "It is to be further urged in defence of the *principle* of confiscation, that in civil conflicts the right of one party to levy upon the other has been generally admitted; that the practice has frequently accorded with the theory; and, what is still more to the purpose, that the royal party and king's generals exercised that right during the struggle. Thus, then, the seizure and confiscation of property in the Revolution was not the act of one side merely, but of both." Sabine, *Loyalist,* I, p. 86.

21. "Though it cannot be denied that the disappearance of the great estates of the aristocratic landlords did result in a somewhat wider distribution of land ownership, it appears that such redistribution of landed wealth was less than has been thought. It is impossible to escape the conclusion that the greater number of those who profited by

the sales of the Commissioners of Forfeitures were well-to-do revolutionists and that the lower classes derived comparatively little immediate benefit." Yoshpe, *Disposition of Loyalist Estates,* p. 117.

22. Paterson, New Jersey, is named after him.

23. Kuntzleman, *Joseph Galloway, Loyalist,* p. 14.

24. "To thousands of South Carolinians, the Revolution became an active issue for the first time in 1780." Smith, *Loyalists and Redcoats,* p. 141.

25. Van Tyne, *The Loyalists in the American Revolution,* p. 250.

26. Now Concord. It was first called by its Indian name of Penacook, but it was Rumford when Benjamin Thompson went there.

27. A fellow passenger on the Channel boat was young Edward Gibbon, historian, who was awed to find himself almost in the presence of one whom he described in his diary as "Mr. Secretary-Colonel-Admiral-Philosopher Thompson."

28. Tyler, *Literary History of the Revolution,* I, p. 135. Jonathan Mayhew has been called the First Unitarian, and it has been said of him that "more clearly than any other man in colonial New England he viewed the fight for 'private judgment' in religion and the fight for personal liberty in politics as one grand battle in which all patriots could join with a will." (Clinton Rossiter, *William and Mary Quarterly,* 3rd series, Vol. VII, no. 4). He bitterly opposed the Stamp Act and was a vigorous proponent of what he called colonial union, a getting-together of the various provinces for the purpose of protecting their rights. He would have been a memorable fighter in the cause of freedom, but he died, at the height of his powers, 9 July 1766.

29. Today a college education is taken for granted, but it was a rare thing in colonial times. Yet of the 1,586 ministers of the Congregational churches in New England during the colonial period only 79 had *not* been graduated

from a college. Bridenbaugh, *Mitre and Sceptre*, pp. 184–85.

30. Callahan, *Royal Raiders*, p. 125.

31. Freeman, *George Washington*, IV, pp. 541–44.

32. Sabine, *Loyalists*, I, p. 49.

33. "While of course among both classes there were shades of opinion which finally met among the neutrals, there is yet one striking difference between the two great groups, whether English or American, whether of the eighteenth or the twentieth century, which constitutes the division between them. Let it be a man of those times, speaking to his friends or his opponents, or let it be an historian of our own day, writing of the crises of the late eighteenth century, the difference between them is on the part of the Tory a preference for authority, grades of society, and a distrust of the common man, and on the part of the Whig a preference for democracy and for liberalism. The difference will last longer than our day. It will show itself even among communists." French, *First Year*, pp. 110–11.

34. Blumenthal, *Camp Followers*, pp. 34–36.

35. Jones, *History of New York during the Revolution*, I, p. 177.

36. Van Tyne, *Loyalists*, p. 255.

37. Serle, *American Journal*, p. 164.

38. It is still not clear how much work he did for Washington's intelligence staff, and there are some historians who believed that he was playing a double game all the while. For a discussion of this, see *William and Mary Quarterly*, 3rd series, volume XVI, pp. 61–72.

39. "Most of all, the Tories were simply unable to cultivate public opinion, to form it and inform it. They showed not a trace of the skill with which, for example, Samuel Adams learned in these years to involve the reading public and the local politicians in a reciprocal catechism of alarms and grievances, of petitions and manifestoes echoed interminably back and forth, from the press to the public to the

press. The Tories were, in fact, afraid of public opinion, afraid of men gathered together, even symbolically, in large numbers. They were afraid, for they felt weak. Here indeed is to be found the basic Tory inhibition during these years of argument, the real and compelling excuse for their apathy. They had ideas, beliefs, values, interests which they were afraid to submit to an American public for approval or rejection. And the weaker they felt themselves to be, the tighter became their allegiance to Britain. The closer they were bound to Britain, the less able were they to support her cause or theirs. So, as the American quarrel with the British government grew more bitter and more deadly, the Tories began slowly, under the guise of loyalty, to sink into a helpless dependence on Britain, an attachment no longer voluntary but growing desperate, and as it became desperate, ceasing to be quite honourable." Nelson, *The American Tory,* pp. 19–20.

40. "Of the two chief classes, the Tories felt that now, when the war had begun, their opponents would rue it. Now would be exerted the might of Great Britain; now avowed rebels would feel the rod; now the supporters of the King would be justified. Military men among the loyalists might look for the chance to do their share of the punishing. In none of the letters of Tories at this time is there any sense that a calamity had happened to them. For themselves they were confident. As for the Whigs, they sat tight, and waited." French, *The First Year,* pp. 110–11.

41. E. C. Bentley's clerihew of course followed much later, though remaining in the spirit of the times:

> George the Third
> Ought never to have occurred.
> One can only wonder
> At so grotesque a blunder.

42. Not all of the German mercenaries brought to America were Hessians. According to Lowell *(The Hessians and Other German Auxiliaries)*, mercenaries numbered 29,166 in all, and of these 5,723 were from Brunswick, 16,992 from Hesse-Cassel, 2,422 from Hesse-Hanau, 1,225 from Waldeck, 1,644 from Anspach, and 1,160 from Anhalt-Zerbst.

43. Davidson, *Propaganda and the American Revolution,* p. 20.

44. *Papers,* Boyd edition, III, p. 117.

44. "He liked his job; he was jealous of his dignity; he quarrelled with other British colonial officials; he was no saint. On the whole, his conduct of Indian affairs in the South before the American Revolution must be regarded as a bright spot in the uneven record of British administration of the American colonies in the later eighteenth century." Alden, *John Stuart,* p. 337.

46. Not Longfellow's Hiawatha, who seems to have been a Chippewa.

47. In World War II the Germans printed false £5, £10, and £20 Bank of England notes, sometimes at the rate of 1,800 an hour. Scott, *Counterfeiting in Colonial America,* p. 12.

48. It was in the southern part of the city, on part of what is now the campus of Trinity College, non-existent then.

49. The Oxford English Dictionary finds the first use of "cow-boy" or "cowboy" in one of Swift's letters to Stella, where it was intended to mean a boy who took care of cows, presumably milch cows. The second meaning, the Oxford finds, was: "A contemptuous appellation applied to some of the tory partisans of Westchester Co., New York, during the Revolutionary War, who were exceedingly barbarous in the treatment of their opponents who favored the American cause." Not until 1882, and then in *Century Magazine,* does

it appear in its present accepted meaning as a hard-riding herder of steers in the West.

50. This structure, which was accidentally burned to the ground St. Patrick's Day of 1892, for many years was a landmark on the river. It was large, white, and handsome. It had been built by Beverly Robinson—the estate was called Beverly, though popularly it was always "the Robinson place"—a Virginian who had married a Phillipse heiress, Mary. Robinson when war came tried to stay neutral, but when he had to choose sides he went with the Loyalists, moving to New York City after it was occupied by the British, where he raised a Loyalist regiment made up largely of friends and dependents. The estate was then expropriated by the Patriots, and the house, conveniently near to West Point, and much more comfortable, was used as a headquarters for the commanding officer of the district. Later it was to be owned and occupied by Henry Brevoort, Washington Irving's ineffable angler, and later still by Hamilton Fish, secretary of state under President Grant.

51. He was to limp for the rest of his life. After one of his destructive raids in Virginia, in his new capacity as a British army brigadier, he asked a Continental prisoner, playfully, what the rebels ever would do with him, Benedict Arnold, if by chance they caught him. The answer was prompt: "We'd cut off the leg that was wounded in the service of your country, and we'd bury it with full military honors, and then we'd hang the rest of you."

52. Now Toms River.

53. *Writings*, XXIV, pp. 263–64.

54. Now the Grenadier Guards.

55. *Writings*, XXV, p. 337.

56. The British had plenty of lieutenant generals in the course of the American Revolution—Gage, Howe, Clinton, Cornwallis, Carleton—but George Washington, the Conti-

nental commander-in-chief, never held a higher rank than that of major general. Not until 1798, after he had ceased to be President and had retired to Mount Vernon, did Washington, under press of a threatened war with France, consent to accept a commission as lieutenant general, and then only on the understanding that he would not be expected to take the field unless in fact war *was* declared; but war wasn't.

57. "Everybody sought to buy on credit, and, on the other hand, when it came to meeting these obligations, it was done, as a rule, in a most unwilling spirit. In going over the county court record for this period, one is led to wonder, in view of the astounding number of cases of book debts that came before the tribune at each session, whether men, as a rule, would pay any indebtedness without taking a chance of relief through the technicalities of the law." Gipson, *Jared Ingersoll*, p. 257.

58. Demond, *The Loyalists in North Carolina*, p. 25.

59. Harrell, *Loyalism in Virginia*, pp. 118–23.

60. Now Portland, Maine.

61. Now Kingston, New York.

62. "Responsibility, loyalty, courage, complacency and priggishness were probably the five main ingredients of George III's character. None of them, separately or in combination, caused him to lose his American Colonies. The forces at work there were much wider than a King or Government could master. But these royal qualities were certainly factors influencing the manner in which Britain faced up to the colonial crisis." Donoughue, *British Politics and the American Revolution*, p. 178.

63. *Letters*, X, p. 392.

64. *Brown, The Good Americans*, p. 188.

65. It had been named not after King George or any other monarch but after a farmer named King, who had

once owned a lot of land near the foot of the "mountain."

66. There were more than 29,000 German mercenaries in the American Revolution, including all reinforcements, and of these only about sixty per cent ever returned to their homeland. Death, whether of disease or in battle, and desertion, claimed the rest. Lowell, *The Hessians and Other German Mercenaries*, p. 300.

Bibliography

ADAIR. DOUGLASS. *See* Oliver, Peter

ADAMS, CHARLES FRANCIS. "Contemporary Opinion on the Howes." *Proceedings of the Massachusetts Historical Society* XLIV (November 1910). Boston: Published by the Society, 1911, pp. 94–120. *See also* Adams, John.

ADAMS, JOHN. *The Works of John Adams, with Life.* Edited by Charles Francis Adams. 10 vols. Boston: Little, Brown & Co., 1850–56.

ADAMS, RANDOLPH G. *Political Ideas of the American Revolution: Britannic-American Contributions to the Problem of Imperial Organization, 1765 to 1775.* New York: Barnes & Noble, Inc., 1958.

ADAMS, SAMUEL. *The Writings of Samuel Adams.* Edited by Harry Alonzo Cushing. 4 vols. New York: G. P. Putnam's Sons, 1904–8.

ALDEN, JOHN RICHARD. *General Gage in America: Being Principally a History of His Role in the American Revolution.* Baton Rouge: Louisiana State University Press, 1948.

——. *John Stuart and the Southern Colonial Frontier: A Study of Indian Relations, War, Trade, and Land Problems in the Southern Wilderness, 1754–1775.* Ann Arbor: University of Michigan Press, 1944.

——. *The South in the Revolution, 1763–1789.* Baton Rouge. Louisiana State University Press, 1957.

ALEXANDER, EDWARD P. *A Revolutionary Conservative: James Duane of New York.* New York: Columbia University Press, 1938.

ANDERSON, GEORGE P. *Ebenezer Mackintosh: Stamp Act Rioter and Patriot.* Publications of the Colonial Society of Massachusetts XXVI.

193

ANDERSON, TROYER STEELE. *The Command of the Howe Brothers during the American Revolution.* New York: Oxford University Press, 1936.

ANDREWS, CHARLES M. *The Colonial Period of American History.* 4 vols. New Haven: Yale University Press, 1966.

AUSTIN, JAMES TRECOTHICK. *The Life of Elbridge Gerry, with Contemporary Letters to the Close of the American Revolution.* 2 vols. Boston: Wealls and Lilly, 1828–29.

BAILYN, BERNARD. *The Ideological Origins of the American Revolution.* Cambridge: Harvard University Press, 1967.

BALDWIN, ALICE M. *The New England Clergy and the American Revolution.* Durham, N.C.: Duke University Press, 1928.

BALDWIN, ERNEST H. "Joseph Galloway, the Loyalist Politician." *Pennsylvania Magazine of History and Biography* XXVI. No. 2 (1902), pp. 161–91, No. 3, 189–321; No. 4, 417–42.

BARGAR, B. D. *Lord Dartmouth and the American Revolution.* Columbia: University of South Carolina Press, 1965.

BASSETT, JOHN S. "The Regulators of North Carolina." American Historical Association *Annual Report,* 1894. Washington: American Historical Association, 1895.

BEACH, STEWART. *Samuel Adams: The Fateful Years, 1764–1776.* New York: Dodd, Mead & Company, 1965.

BEARDSLEY, EBEN EDWARDS. *Life and Correspondence of the Right Reverend Samuel Seabury, D.D.* Boston: Houghton Mifflin & Co., 1881.

BECKER, CARL. *The Eve of the Revolution: a Chronicle of the Breach with England.* New Haven: Yale University Press, 1918.

BEER, GEORGE LOUIS. *British Colonial Policy, 1754–1765.* New York: The Macmillan Company, 1907.

———. *British Politics and the American Revolution: The Path to War, 1773–75.* New York: The Macmillan Company, 1907.

———. *The Commercial Policy of England toward the American Colonies.* New York: Columbia University Press, 1893.

BELCHER, HENRY. *The First American Civil War.* 2 vols. London: Macmillan & Co. Ltd., 1911.

BENTON, WILLIAM ALLEN. *Whig-Loyalism: An Aspect of Political Ideology in the American Revolutionary Era.* Rutherford, Madison, Teaneck, N.J.: Fairleigh Dickinson University Press, 1969.

BEZANSON, ANNE, AND ASSOCIATES. *Prices and Inflation During the American Revolution: Pennsylvania, 1770–90.* Philadelphia: University of Pennsylvania Press, 1951.

BILLIAS, GEORGE ATHAN, editor. *The American Revolution: How Revolutionary Was It?* New York: Holt, Rinehart & Winston, Inc., 1965.

BISHOP, CORTLANDT F. *History of Elections in the American Colonies.* New York: Columbia University Press, 1893.

BLIVEN, BRUCE, JR. *Under the Guns: New York, 1775–76.* New York: Harper & Row, 1972.

BOORSTIN, DANIEL J. *The Americans: The Colonial Experience.* New York: Random House, 1958.

BOYD, JULIAN P. *Anglo-American Union: Joseph Galloway's Plans to Preserve the British Empire, 1774–1788.* Philadelphia: University of Pennsylvania Press, 1941. *See also* Jefferson, Thomas.

BRENNAN, ELLEN ELIZABETH. *Plural Office-Holding in Massachusetts, 1760–1780: Its Relation to the "Separation" of Departments of Government.* Chapel Hill: The University of North Carolina Press, 1945.

BRIDENBAUGH, CARL. *Mitre and Sceptre: Transatlantic Faiths, Ideas, Personalities, and Politics, 1689–1775.* New York: Oxford University Press, 1962.

BRINTON, CRANE. *The Anatomy of Revolution.* New York: W. W. Norton & Company, Inc., 1938.

BROWN, GERALD SAXON. *The American Secretary: The Colonial Policy of Lord George Germain, 1775–1778.* Ann Arbor: University of Michigan Press, 1963.

BROWN, RICHARD MAXWELL. *The South Carolina Regulators: The Story of the First American Vigilante Movement.* Cambridge: Harvard University Press, 1963.

BROWN, ROBERT E. *Middle-Class Democracy and the Revolution in Massachusetts, 1691–1780.* Ithaca, N.Y.: Cornell University Press, 1955.

BROWN, WALLACE. "The American Loyalists." *History Today* XII, No. 3 (March 1962), pp. 147–57.

————. *The Good Americans: The Loyalists in the American Revolution.* New York: William Morrow and Co., Inc., 1969.

————. *The King's Friends: The Composition and Motives of the American Loyalist Claimants.* Providence: Brown University Press, 1965.

————. "A View at Two Hundred Years: Loyalists in the American Revolution." *Proceedings of the American Antiquarian Society* 80 (1971), pp. 25–47. Worcester, Mass.

BROWN, WELDON A. *Empire or Independence: A Study in the Failure of Reconciliation, 1774–1783.* Baton Rouge: Louisiana State University Press, 1941.

BRUNHOUSE, ROBERT T. *The Counter-Revolution in Pennsylvania, 1776–1790.* Harrisburg, Pa.: Pennsylvania Historical Commission, 1942.

BULLOCK, CHARLES J. *The Finances of the United States from 1775 to 1789, with Especial Reference to the Budget.* Madison: University of Wisconsin Press, 1895.

BUTTERFIELD, HERBERT. *George III and the Historians.* New York: The Macmillan Company, 1959.

————. *George III, Lord North, and the People, 1779–80.* London: G. Bell and Sons, Ltd., 1949.

BUTTERFIELD, L. H., editor. *Letters of Benjamin Rush.* 2 vols. Princeton: Princeton University Press, 1951.

CALLAHAN, NORTH. *Flight from the Republic: The Tories of the American Revolution.* Indianapolis: The Bobbs-Merrill Company, Inc., 1967.

————. *Royal Raiders: The Tories of the American Revolution.* Indianapolis: The Bobbs-Merrill Company, 1963.

CAMPBELL, CHARLES A. "Robinson's House in the Hudson Highlands." *The Magazine of American History* IV. Chicago and New York: A. and S. Barnes Company, 1880.

CAMPBELL, WILLIAM W. *The Border Warfare of New York during the Revolution; or, The Annals of Tryon County, New York.* New York: Baker and Scribner, 1849.

CARTER, CLARENCE EDWIN. *See* Gage, Thomas

CHAMPION, RICHARD. *The American Correspondence of a Bristol*

Merchant, 1766–1776. Edited by G. H. Guttrudge. Berkeley: University of California Press, 1934.

CHANNING, EDWARD. *A History of the United States,* 6 vols. New York: The Macmillan Company, 1925.

CHRISTIE, IAN R. *Crisis of Empire: Great Britain and the American Colonies, 1754–1783.* New York: W. W. Norton & Company, Inc., 1966.

————. *The End of North's Ministry, 1780–1782.* London: Macmillan & Co., Ltd., 1958.

CLARK, DORA MAE. *British Opinion and the American Revolution.* New Haven: Yale University Press, 1930.

CLARK, GEORGE LARKIN. *Silas Deane, a Connecticut Leader in the American Revolution.* New York and London: G. P. Putnam's Sons, 1913.

CLARKE, MARY PATTERSON. *Parliamentary Privilege in the American Colonies.* New Haven: Yale University Press, 1943.

CLINTON, SIR HENRY. *The American Rebellion: Sir Henry Clinton's Narrative of His Campaigns, 1775–1782, with an Appendix of Original Documents.* Edited by William B. Willcox. New Haven: Yale University Press, 1954.

COLBOURN, H. TREVOR. *The Lamp of Experience: Whig History and the Intellectual Origins of the American Revolution.* Chapel Hill: University of North Carolina Press, 1965.

CORWIN, EDWARD S. *French Policy and the American Alliance of 1778.* Princeton: Princeton University Press, 1916.

COUPLAND, REGINALD. *The American Revolution and the British Empire.* London: Longmans, Green and Co., 1930.

COUPLAND, RICHARD. *The Quebec Act: A Study in Statesmanship.* Oxford: Oxford University Press, 1925.

CRARY, CATHERINE SNELL. "The Tory and the Spy: The Double Life of James Rivington." *William and Mary Quarterly,* 3rd volume XVI (1959), pp. 61–72.

CRESSWELL, NICHOLAS. *Journal.* New York: The Dial Press, 1928.

CROSS, A. L. *The Anglican Episcopate and the American Colonies.* New York: Longmans, Green and Co., 1902.

CUSHING, HARRY ALONZO. *See* ADAMS, SAMUEL

DAVIDSON, ELIZABETH H. *The Establishment of the English*

Church in Continental American Colonies. Durham, N.C.: Duke University Press, 1936.

DAVIDSON, PHILIP. *Propaganda and the American Revolution, 1763–1783.* Chapel Hill: University of North Carolina Press, 1941.

DAVIS, RICH DEWEY. *Financial History of the United States.* New York: Longmans, Green and Co., 1925.

DAWSON, HENRY BARTON, editor. *New York City during the American Revolution: a Collection of Original Papers.* New York: Mercantile Library Association, 1861.

DEANE, SILAS. *The Silas Deane Papers.* 5 vols. New York: The New-York Historical Society, 1887–91.

DEMOND, ROBERT O. *The Loyalists in North Carolina during the Revolution.* Hamden, Conn.: Archon Books, 1964.

DICKERSON, OLIVER MORTON. *American Colonial Government, 1696–1765: A Study of the British Board of Trade in its Relation to the American Colonies, Political, Industrial, Administrative.* Cleveland: The Arthur H. Clark Company, 1912.

———. Editor. *Boston under Military Rule, 1768–1769.* Boston: Chapman & Grimes, 1936.

———. *The Navigation Acts and the American Revolution.* Philadelphia: University of Pennsylvania Press, 1951.

DONOUGHUE, BERNARD. *British Politics and the American Revolution: The Path to War, 1773–75.* London: Macmillan & Co., Ltd., 1964.

DOUGLASS, ELISHA P. *Rebels and Democrats: The Struggle for Equal Political Rights and Majority Rule During the American Revolution.* Chapel Hill: University of North Carolina Press, 1955.

EGERTON, H. E. *The Causes and Character of the American Revolution.* London: Oxford University Press, 1923.

EINSTEIN, CAVIS. *Divided Loyalties: Americans in England during the War of Independence.* London: Cobden-Sanderson, 1933.

ELLIS, GEORGE E. "Governor Thomas Hutchinson." *Atlantic Monthly,* May 1884, pp. 266–69.

ELLIS, GEORGE EDWARD. *The Sentiment of Independence: Its Growth and Consummation.* Boston: Houghton Mifflin and Company, 1888.

FARRAND, MAX. "The Taxation of Tea, 1767–1773." *American Historical Review* III, pp. 266–69.

FISHER, SIDNEY GEORGE. "The Legendary and Myth-Making Process in Histories of the American Revolution." *Proceedings of the American Philosophical Society* LI, No. 204 (April-June 1912).

———. *The Struggle for American Independence.* 2 vols. Philadelphia: J. B. Lippincott Company, 1909.

FITZPATRICK, JOHN C. *See* WASHINGTON, GEORGE

FLEXNER, JAMES THOMAS. *The Traitor and the Spy: Benedict Arnold and John André.* New York: Harcourt, Brace and Company, 1953.

FLICK, ALEXANDER CLARENCE. *Loyalism in New York during the American Revolution.* New York: Columbia University Press, 1901.

FORD, WORTHINGTON CHAUNCEY, editor. *Boston in 1775.* Brooklyn: Historical Printing Club, 1892.

———. "Parliament and the Howes." *Proceedings of the Massachusetts Historical Society* XLIV (November 1910), pp. 120–44.

FREEMAN, DOUGLAS SOUTHALL. *George Washington: A Biography.* 6 vols. New York: Charles Scribner's Sons, 1948–54.

FRENCH, ALLEN. *The First Year of the American Revolution.* Boston: Houghton Mifflin Company, 1934.

———. *General Gage's Informers: New Material Upon Lexington and Concord, Benjamin Thompson as Loyalist and the Treachery of Benjamin Church, Jr.* Ann Arbor: University of Michigan Press, 1932.

FROTHINGHAM, RICHARD. *The Rise of the Republic of the United States.* Boston: Little, Brown & Co., 1910.

GAGE, THOMAS. *The Correspondence of General Thomas Gage with the Secretaries of State, 1763–1775.* Compiled and edited by Clarence Edwin Carter. 2 vols. New Haven: Yale University Press, 1931.

Gipson, Lawrence Henry. *The Coming of the American Revolution, 1763–1775*. New York: Harper & Brothers, 1954.

———. *Jared Ingersoll: a Study of American Loyalism in Relation to British Colonial Government*. New Haven: Yale University Press, 1920.

Goodman, Nathan Gerson. *Benjamin Rush, Physician and Citizen, 1746–1813*. Philadelphia: University of Pennsylvania Press, 1934.

Goodnough, David. *The Cherry Valley Massacre, November 11, 1778: The Frontier Atrocity That Shocked a Young Nation*. New York: Franklin Watts, Inc., 1968.

Granger, Bruce Ingram. *Political Satire in the American Revolution, 1763–1783*. Ithaca, N.Y.: Cornell University Press, 1960.

Graymont, Barbara. *The Iroquois in the American Revolution*. Syracuse, N.Y.: Syracuse University Press, 1972.

Greene, Evarts Boutell. *The Revolutionary Generation, 1763–1790*. New York: The Macmillan Company, 1943.

Greene, Jack P., and Jellison, Richard M. "The Currency Act of 1764 in Imperial-Colonial Relations, 1764–1776." *William and Mary Quarterly*, 3rd series, XVIII, No. 4.

Gruber, Ira D. "Lord Howe and Lord George Germain: British Politics and the Winning of American Independence." *William and Mary Quarterly*, 3rd series XXII, No. 2 (April 1965).

Guttrudge, G. H. *See* Champion, Richard

Haight, C. *Before the Coming of the Loyalists*. Toronto: Haight & Company, 1897.

Hale, Edward Everett, and Hale, Edward E., Jr. *Franklin in France*. Boston: Roberts Brothers, 1887.

Hamer, Philip M. "John Stuart's Indian Policy during the Early Months of the American Revolution." *Mississippi Valley Historical Review* XVII, No. 3 (December 1930), pp. 351–66.

Harlow, Ralph Volney. *Samuel Adams, Promoter of the American Revolution: A Study in Psychology and Politics*. New York: Henry Holt and Company, 1923.

Harrell, Isaac S. *Loyalism in Virginia: Chapters in the Economic*

History of the Revolution. Durham, N.C.: Duke University Press, 1926.

HARRINGTON, VIRGINIA D. *The New York Merchant on the Eve of the Revolution.* New York: Columbia University Press, 1935.

HEADLEY, J. T. *The Chaplains and Clergy of the Revolution.* New York: Charles Scribner, 1864.

HENDERSON, ARCHIBALD. "The Origin of the Regulation in North Carolina." *American Historical Review* XXI (1915–1916).

HICKHOUSE, FRED JUNKIN. *The Preliminaries of the American Revolution as Seen in the English Press.* New York: Columbia University Press, 1926.

HOSMER, J. K. *The Life of Thomas Hutchinson, Royal Governor of the Province of Massachusetts Bay.* Boston: Houghton, Mifflin & Co., 1896.

————. *Samuel Adams.* Boston: Houghton, Mifflin & Co., 1885.

HOWARD, GEORGE ELLIOTT. *Preliminaries of the American Revolution.* New York: Harper & Brothers, 1905.

HULTON, ANN. *Letters of a Loyalist Lady: Being the Letters of Ann Hulton, sister of Henry Hulton, Commissioner of Customs at Boston, 1767–1776.* Cambridge: Harvard University Press, 1927.

HUNT, AGNES. *The Provincial Committees of Safety of the American Revolution.* Cleveland, Ohio: Winn & Judson, 1904.

HUTCHINSON, PETER ORLANDO, editor. *The Diary and Letters of His Excellency Thomas Hutchinson, Esq.* 2 vols. Boston: Houghton, Mifflin & Co., 1886.

INGRAHAM, EDWARD D. *Papers in Relation to the Case of Silas Deane.* Philadelphia: T. K. and P. G. Collins, 1855.

JAMESON, J. FRANKLIN. *The American Revolution considered as a Social Movement.* Princeton: Princeton University Press, 1926.

JEFFERSON, THOMAS. *The Papers of Thomas Jefferson.* 18 volumes. Edited by Julian P. Boyd. Princeton: Princeton University Press, 1951.

JELLISON, RICHARD M. *See* GREENE, JACK P.

JONES, THOMAS. *History of New York during the Revolutionary*

War, and of the Leading Events in the Other Colonies at that Period. 2 vols. New York: The New-York Historical Society, 1879.

KEESEY, RUTH M. "Loyalism in Bergen County, New Jersey." *William and Mary Quarterly*, 3rd series, XVIII, No. 4.

KLINGELHOFER, HERBERT E. "Matthew Ridley's Diary during the Peace Negotiations of 1782." *William and Mary Quarterly*, 3rd series, XX, No. 1.

KNOLLENBERG, BERNHARD. "Benjamin Franklin and the Hutchinson and Oliver Letters." *Yale University Library Gazette*, 47, No. I (July 1972).

———. *Origin of the American Revolution, 1759–1766.* New York: The Macmillan Company, 1960.

KUNTZLEMAN, OLIVER C. *Joseph Galloway, Loyalist.* Philadelphia: Temple University, 1941.

LABAREE, BENJAMIN W. *The Boston Tea Party.* New York: Oxford University Press, 1964.

LABAREE, LEONARD WOODS. *Conservatism in Early American History.* New York: New York University Press, 1948.

———. "The Nature of American Loyalism." *Proceedings of the American Antiquarian Society*, 54 (1945); pp. 15–58. Worcester, Mass.

———. *Royal Government in America: A Study of the British Colonial System before 1783.* New York: Frederick Ungar Publishing Co., 1958.

LACY, DAN. *The Meaning of the American Revolution.* New York: New American Library, 1964.

LANCTOT, GUSTAVE. *Canada & the American Revolution, 1774–1783.* Cambridge: Harvard University Press, 1967.

LECKY, W. E. H. *History of England in the Eighteenth Century*, 8 vols. London: Longmans, Green & Co., 1878–90.

LEE, CHARLES. *Memoirs of the Life of Richard Henry Lee, and His Correspondence.* 2 vols. Philadelphia: H. C. Carey and I. Lea, 1825.

LEIBY, ADRIAN C. *The Revolutionary War in the Hackensack Valley, The Jersey Dutch and the Neutral Ground, 1775–*

1783. New Brunswick, N.J.: Rutgers University Press, 1962.

LOCKE, GEORGE HERBERT. *The Queen's Ranger*. Toronto: The Public Library of Toronto, 1923.

LOWELL, EDWARD J. *The Hessians and the Other German Auxiliaries of Great Britain in the Revolutionary War*. New York: Harper & Brothers, 1884.

LUTNICK, SOLOMON. *The American Revolution and the British Press, 1775–1783*. Columbia: University of Missouri Press, 1967.

LYND, STAUGHTON. "Who Should Rule at Home? Dutchess County, New York, in the American Revolution." *William and Mary Quarterly*, 3rd series, XVIII, No. 3.

MACKALL, LEONARD L. "A Letter from John Randolph to Thomas Jefferson." *Proceedings of the American Antiquarian Society*, New Series, 30, pp. 17–31.

MACKESY, PIERS. *The War for America, 1775–1783*. Cambridge: Harvard University Press, 1964.

MAIER, PAULINE. *From Resistance to Revolution: Colonial Radicals and the Development of American Opposition to Britain, 1765–1776*. New York: Alfred A. Knopf, 1972.

MAIN, JACKSON TURNER. "Government by the People: The American Revolution and the Democratization of the Legislatures." *William and Mary Quarterly*, 3rd series, XXIII (July 1966), pp. 391–408.

———. *Rebel Versus Tory: The Crisis of the Revolution, 1773–1776*. Chicago: Rand McNally & Company, 1963.

———. *The Social Structure of Revolutionary America*. Princeton: Princeton University Press, 1965.

MANROSS, WILLIAM WILSON. *A History of the American Episcopal Church*. New York and Milwaukee: Morehouse Publishing Company, 1935.

MAYO, KATHERINE. *General Washington's Dilemma*. New York: Harcourt, Brace and Company, 1938.

METZGER, CHARLES H. *The Quebec Act: A Primary Cause of the American Revolution*. New York: The United States Catholic Historical Society, 1936.

MILLER, HUNTER, editor. *Treaties and Other International Acts of the United States of America.* 8 vols. Washington: Government Printing Office, 1931.

MILLER, JOHN C. *Origins of the American Revolution.* Boston: Little, Brown and Company, 1943.

————. *Sam Adams, Pioneer in Propaganda.* Boston: Little, Brown and Company, 1936.

MILLER, PERRY. *The New England Mind.* New York: The Macmillan Company, 1939.

MORGAN, EDMUND S. *The Birth of the Republic, 1763–89.* Chicago: University of Chicago Press, 1956.

————. "Thomas Hutchinson and the Stamp Act." *New England Quarterly* December 1948, pp. 459–92.

———— and MORGAN, HELEN M. *The Stamp Act Crisis: Prologue to Revolution.* Chapel Hill: University of North Carolina Press, 1953.

MORRIS, RICHARD B., editor. *The Era of the American Revolution.* New York: Columbia University Press, 1939.

————. *The Peacemakers: The Great Powers and American Independence.* New York: Harper & Row, 1965.

MURRAY, SIR JAMES. *Letters from America, 1773 to 1780.* Edited by Eric Robson. Manchester: Manchester University Press, 1951.

NAMIER, LEWIS. *England in the Age of the American Revolution.* London: Macmillan & Company, Ltd., 1930.

NELSON, W. H. "The Last Hopes of the American Loyalists." *Canadian Historical Review* XXXII, No. 1 (March 1951), pp. 22–43.

NELSON, WILLIAM H. *The American Tory.* Oxford: The Clarendon Press, 1961.

NEVINS, ALLAN. *The American States During and After the Revolution, 1775–1798.* New York: The Macmillan Company, 1927.

NORTON, MARY BETH. *The British-Americans: The Loyalist Exiles in England, 1774–1789.* Boston: Little, Brown & Company, 1972.

OBERHOLTZER, ELLIS PAXSON. *Robert Morris: Patriot and Financier.* New York: The Macmillan Company, 1903.

OLIVER, PETER. *Origin and Progress of the American Rebellion: A Tory View.* Edited by Douglass Adair and John A. Schutz. San Marino, Calif.: The Huntington Library, 1961.

PALMER, ROBERT ROSWELL. *The Age of the Democratic Revolution: A Political History of Europe and America, 1760–1800.* 2 vols. Princeton: Princeton University Press, 1964.

PARES, RICHARD. *King George III and the Politicians.* New York: Oxford University Press, 1953.

PEABODY, ANDREW PRESTON. "Boston Mobs before the Revolution." *Atlantic Monthly* LXII (September 1888), pp. 321–33.

PECK, EPAPHRODITUS. *The Loyalists of Connecticut.* New Haven: Yale University Press, 1934.

PENNYPACKER, MORTON. *General Washington's Spies on Long Island and in New York.* Brooklyn: Long Island Historical Society, 1939.

PICKERING, OCTAVIUS. *See* UPHAM, CHARLES WENTWORTH

RITCHESON, CHARLES R. *British Politics and the American Revolution.* Norman: University of Oklahoma Press, 1954.

ROBSON, ERIC. *The American Revolution in its Political and Military Aspects, 1763–1783.* London: The Batchworth Press, 1955. *See also* MURRAY, SIR JAMES

ROSEMAN, KENNETH R. *Thomas Mifflin and the Politics of the American Revolution.* Chapel Hill: University of North Carolina Press, 1952.

ROSSITER, CLINTON. *Seedtime of the Republic: The Origin of the American Tradition of Political Liberty.* New York: Harcourt, Brace & Co., 1953.

ROWLAND, KATE MASON. *The Life of Charles Carroll of Carrollton, 1737–1832.* 2 vols. New York and London: G. P. Putnam's Sons, 1899.

RUDE, GEORGE. *The Crowd in History: A Study of Popular Disturbances in France and England, 1730–1848.* New York: John Wiley & Sons, Inc., 1964.

———. *Wilkes and Liberty: A Social Study of 1763 to 1774.* London: Oxford University Press, 1962.

RUMFORD, COUNT. *See* THOMPSON, BENJAMIN

SABINE, LORENZO. *Biographical Sketches of Loyalists of the Ameri-*

can Revolution. 2 vols. Boston: Little, Brown and Company, 1864.

SARGENT, WINTHROP. *Life and Career of Major André.* Boston: Ticknor and Fields, 1861.

SCHLESINGER, ARTHUR MEIER. "The American Revolution Reconsidered." *Political Science Quarterly* XXXIV, pp. 61–78.

———. *The Colonial Merchants and the American Revolution.* New York: The Facsimile Library, Inc., 1939.

———. *Prelude to Independence: The Newspaper War in Britain.* New York: Alfred A. Knopf, Inc., 1958.

SCHUTZ, JOHN A. *See* OLIVER, PETER

SCOTT, KENNETH. *Counterfeiting in Colonial America.* New York: Oxford University Press, 1957.

SEABURY, REV. SAMUEL. *Letters of a Westchester Farmer (1774–1775).* Edited and with an introduction by Clarence H. Vance. White Plains, N.Y.: Westchester County Historical Society, 1930.

SELLERS, CHARLES COLEMAN. *Benedict Arnold, the Proud Warrior.* New York: Minton, Balch and Company, 1930.

SERLE, AMBROSE. *The American Journal of Ambrose Serle, Secretary to Lord Howe, 1776–1778.* Edited by Edward H. Tatum, Jr. San Marino, Calif.: The Huntington Library, 1940.

SHY, JOHN W. "A New Look at Colonial Militia." *William and Mary Quarterly,* 3rd series, XX, No. 2.

———. *Toward Lexington: The Role of the British Army in the Coming of the American Revolution.* Princeton: Princeton University Press, 1965.

SIEBERT, WILBUR H. *The Exodus of the Loyalists from Penobscot to Passamaquoddy.* Columbus: Ohio State University Press, 1914.

———. *The Legacy of the American Revolution to the British West Indies and Bahamas.* Columbus: Ohio State University Press, 1913.

———. *The Loyalist Refugees of New Hampshire.* Columbus: Ohio State University Press, 1916.

———. *The Loyalists and Six Nation Indians in the Niagara Peninsula.* Ottawa: Royal Society of Canada, 1915.

————. *The Refugee Loyalists of Connecticut.* Ottawa: Royal Society of Canada, 1916.

SMITH, PAUL H. *Loyalists and Redcoats: A Study in British Revolutionary Policy.* Chapel Hill: University of North Carolina Press, 1964.

SOSIN, JACK M. *Agents and Merchants: British Colonial Policy and the Origins of the American Revolution, 1763–1775.* Lincoln: University of Nebraska Press, 1965.

SPECTOR, MARGARET MARION. *The American Department of the British Government, 1768–1782.* New York: Columbia University Press, 1940.

STARK, JAMES H. *The Loyalists of Massachusetts and the Other Side of the American Revolution.* Boston: James H. Stark, 1910.

STILLE, CHARLES J. *The Life and Times of John Dickinson, 1732–1808.* Philadelphia: Historical Society of Pennsylvania, 1891.

STOCKBRIDGE, J. C. "The Case of Major André." *Magazine of American History* III, part II.

SUMNER, CHARLES GRAHAM. *The Financier and the Finances of the American Revolution.* 2 vols. New York: Dodd, Mead and Co., 1891.

SUTHERLAND, STELLA H. *Population Distribution in Colonial America.* New York: Columbia University Press, 1956.

SWEET, WILLIAM WARREN. *Religion in Colonial America.* New York: Charles Scribner's Sons, 1942.

SWIGGETT, HOWARD. *War Out of Niagara: Walter Butler and the Tory Rangers.* Port Washington, N.Y.: Ira J. Friedman, Inc., 1963.

TATUM, EDWARD H., JR. *See* SERLE, AMBROSE

THOMPSON, BENJAMIN. *The Complete Works of Count Rumford.* 4 vols. Boston: The American Academy of Arts and Sciences, 1870.

THORNTON, JOHN WINGATE. *The Pulpit of the American Revolution.* Boston: Gould and Lincoln, 1860.

TIFFANY, C. C. *A History of the Protestant Episcopal Church in the United States of America.* New York: Charles Scribner's Sons, 1899.

TREVELYAN, GEORGE OTTO. *The American Revolution.* 6 vols. London: Longmans, Green & Co., 1905.

TRUMBULL, JOHN. *Autobiography, Reminiscences and Letters, from 1756 to 1841.* New Haven, Conn.: B. L. Hamlen, 1841.

TYLER, MOSES COIT. *The Literary History of the American Revolution.* 2 vols. New York: G. P. Putnam's Sons, 1897.

————. "The Party of the Loyalists in the American Revolution." *American Historical Review,* October 1895.

UPHAM, CHARLES WENTWORTH, and PICKERING, OCTAVIUS. *The Life of Timothy Pickering.* 4 vols. Boston: Little, Brown and Co., 1891.

VAN DOREN, CARL. *Secret History of the American Revolution.* New York: The Viking Press, 1941.

VAN TYNE, CLAUDE HALSTEAD. *England and America: Rivals in the American Revolution.* Cambridge: Cambridge University Press, 1929.

————. *The Loyalists in the American Revolution.* New York: Peter Smith, 1929.

VER STEEG, CLARENCE L. *Robert Morris: Revolutionary Financier.* Philadelphia: University of Pennsylvania Press, 1954.

WALLACE, WILLARD M. *Traitorous Hero: The Life and Fortunes of Benedict Arnold.* New York: Harper & Brothers, 1954.

WALSH, RICHARD. *Charleston's Sons of Liberty: A Study of the Artisans, 1763–1789.* Columbia: University of South Carolina Press, 1959.

WASHINGTON, GEORGE. *The Writings of George Washington, from the Original Manuscript Sources, 1745–1799.* Edited by John C. Fitzpatrick. 39 vols. Washington, D.C.: Government Printing Office, 1931–44.

WELLS, WILLIAM VINCENT. *The Life and Public Services of Samuel Adams.* Boston: Little, Brown and Company, 1865.

WICKWIRE, FRANKLIN B. "John Pownall and British Colonial Policy." *William and Mary Quarterly,* 3rd series, XX, No. 4.

WILLCOX, WILLIAM B. *See* CLINTON, SIR HENRY

WINSOR, JUSTIN. *Narrative and Critical History of America.* 6 vols. Boston: Houghton Mifflin Company, 1887.

WINSTANLEY, D. A. *Lord Chatham and the Whig Opposition.* Cambridge: Cambridge University Press, 1912.

WOOD, GORDON S. "A Note on Mobs in the American Revolution." *William and Mary Quarterly,* 3rd series, XXIII (October 1966), pp. 635–43.

WRONG, GEORGE M. *Canada and the American Revolution: The Disruption of the First British Empire.* New York: The Macmillan Company, 1935.

YOSHPE, HARRY B. *The Disposition of Loyalist Estates in the Southern District of the State of New York.* New York: Columbia University Press, 1939.

ZEICHNER, OSCAR. *Connecticut's Years of Controversy, 1750–1776.* Chapel Hill: University of North Carolina Press, 1949.

Index

A

Adams, Henry, 13
Adams, John, 6, 13, 32, 43, 44, 157, 161; note 5
Adams, John Quincy, 156
Adams, Samuel, 10–14, 17, 21, 22, 32, 39, 43, 44, 61, 96–98; notes 5, 7, 39
Adams, Samuel (deacon), 13
Adams, Dr. William, 156
André, Major John, 132, 134, 136, 139, 140, 141, 149, 152
Arnold, Benedict, 50, 126, 132, 134, 136–39, 140, 141, 177; note 51
Asgill, Capt. Charles, 151, 152, 153
Asgill, Lady, 151, 152, 153

B

Barras, Comte de, 150, 151
Barre, Col. Isaac, 27, 28, 29, 30; note 11
Barrington, Lord, 9
Beach, Rev. John, 87
Bernard, Gov. Francis, 9, 16, 18, 21, 22
Boston Tea Party, 22, 33
Boucher, Rev. Jonathan, 90
Braddock, Gen. Edward, 115
Brant, Joseph, 125
Bull, Lt. Gov. William, 2
Bunker Hill, 43, 76, 161, 169
Burgoyne, Gen. John, 67, 112, 167, 177
Burke, Edmund, 27 125
Byles, Rev. Mather, 90, 91

C

Campbell, Gov. William, 122, 123
Carleton, Gen. Sir Guy, 105, 149, 152
Carlyle, Lord. *See* Howard, Frederick
Carroll, Charles, 4
Chambers, Col. James, 68
Church, Dr. Benjamin, 44, 46–49, 50, 74, 89
Clay, Henry, 156
Clinton, Gen. Sir Henry, 69, 137, 147–49, 152, 178
Clossy, Dr. Samuel, 91
Colbert, James, 122
Cooper, Rev. Myles, 91
Coote, Capt. Eyre, 152
Cornwallis, Lord, 152
Curwen, Samuel, 175, 180

D

Daggett, Naphtali, 31
Dartmouth, Lord, 26
Dawes, William, Jr., 43
De Lancey, Oliver, 167
De Peyster, Capt. Abraham, 171
Deveaux, Col. Andrew, 65, 66, 177
Dickinson, John, 57–59, 110, 157
Duche, Rev. Jacob, 88, 89, 90
Dulany, Daniel, 2, 110
Dunbar, Capt. Moses, 130

E

Eden, Gov. Robert, 167

210

Edwards, Stephen, 146

F

Fairfax, Lord, 63
Fanning, Col. David, 167
Ferdinand, Prince, of Brunswick, 76
Ferguson, Col. Patrick, 169
Fleeming, John, 39, 40, 46
Flucker, Lucy, 2
Flucker, Thomas, 3, 176
Fox, Charles James, 164
Franklin, Benjamin, 2, 30, 54, 55, 59, 60, 80, 103, 146, 147, 157, 161; note 13
Franklin, Gov. William, 2, 107, 146, 147, 167
Franklin, William Temple, 2, 147

G

Gage, Gen. Thomas, 24, 48, 49, 73, 75, 99
Gallatin, Albert, 156
Galloway, Joseph, 57–59, 60, 61, 102, 166, 167
Galvez, Gov. Bernardo de, 66
Gambier, Lord, 156
Gates, Gen. Horatio, 67, 129
George III, 21, 24, 26, 60, 61, 64, 78, 86, 107–9, 172, 181
Germain, Lord, 68, 76, 77, 157
Gordon, Major James, 151–53
Goulburn, Henry, 156
Graham, Lt. Gov. John, 65
Granville, Lord, 63
Grasse, Admiral Comte de, 150, 151
Greene, Gen. Nathanael, 47, 65
Greenleaf, Sheriff, 18, 36

H

Hale, Nathan, 130
Hallowell, Benjamin, 18, 20
Hamilton, Alexander, 137
Hancock, John, 4, 43
Hardwicke, Lord, 26
Hazen, Brig. Gen. Moses, 148–51
Heath, Gen. William, 115

Henry, Patrick, 144, 159
Heyward, Thomas, 2
Hillsborough, Lord, 24, 26
Hood, Zachariah, 33
Hopkins, Francis, 88
Howard, Frederick, 5th Earl of Carlyle, 66, 67
Howe, Admiral Lord Richard, 99
Howe, Gen. Sir William, 60, 61, 75, 90, 99, 100, 102, 128, 129, 145, 152, 178
Huddy, Joshua, 145–48, 153
Hutchinson, Anne, 9
Hutchinson, Gov. Thomas, 8, 9, 10, 14, 16–18, 20, 21, 24, 26, 54, 61, 83, 107; note 8

I

Ingersoll, Jared, 30, 31
Inglis, Rev. Charles, 87, 88

J

Jameson, Lt. Col. John, 134, 137
Jay, John, 157, 162
Jefferson, Thomas, 58, 109, 113, 129, 159
Johnson, Sir John, 126, 127, 167
Johnson, Sir William, 124–26
Jones, Judge Thomas, 100

K

Key, Philip Barton, 180
King's Mountain, Battle of, 84, 169; note 65
Knox, Gen. Henry, 2, 3, 75, 137, 176

L

Lafayette, Marquis de, 67, 126, 137
Laurens, Henry, 158, 159
Laurens, John, 158
Lavoisier, Antoine Laurent, 79
Lee, Gen. Charles, 157
Lee, Richard Henry, 30
Lippincott, Capt. Richard, 147–49
Luzerne, Chevalier de La, 137

M

McGillivray, Alexander, 122
McIntosh, William, 122
Mackintosh, Ebenezer, 18, 21
Malcolm, John, 32
Mansfield, Lord, 26
Maximilian, Prince, of Zweibrucken, 78, 79
Mayhew, Rev. Jonathan, 82, 83
Mein, John, 39, 40, 46
Montgomery, Gen. Richard, 126
Morris, Robert, 65
Muhlenberg, Rev. John Peter Gabriel, 91, 92

N

North, Lord, 26, 61, 157, 162, 164

O

Odell, Rev. Jonathan, 141
Oliver, Andrew, 10, 17, 18, 22

P

Paine, Thomas, 108, 109, 129
Paterson, William, 64; note 22
Paulding, John, 132, 134, 140
Paxton, Charles, 20
Penn, William, 53, 58
Pitt, William, 28, 100, 125; note 13
Polk, Ezekial, 181
Polk, James K., 180
Pomeroy, Gen. Seth, 115
Pontiac, 119
Prescott, Col. William, 43
Putnam, Gen. Isaac, 43, 115

R

Randolph, Edmund, 113
Randolph, John, 113
Revere, Paul, 43, 44
Richard I, King of England, 36
Richardson, Ebenezer, 32, 33
Rivington, James, 89, 93, 95, 96, 99, 100, 102, 103, 105

Robertson, Gen. James, 102, 149, 152
Rochambeau, Comte de, 150, 151
Rockingham, Marquis of, 26, 162
Ross, Aeneas, 87
Ross, Betsy, 87
Ruggles, Gen. Timothy, 2, 75
Rumford, Baron. *See* Thompson, Benjamin
Rumford, Mme. Lavoisier de, 78, 80
Rush, Dr. Benjamin, 42
Russell, Jonathan, 156

S

Schaack, Capt. John, 152
Schuyler, Gen. Philip, 4
Seabury, Rev. Samuel, 88
Sears, Isaac ("King"), 95
Sewell, Jonathan, 1
Shelbourne, Lord, 162, 164
Skene, Philip, 167
Sneider, Christopher, 33
Spencer, Gen. Joseph, 115
Stamp Act, 16, 17, 20, 28, 29, 30, 32; note 28
Stansbury, Joseph, 141
Story, William, 20
Stuart, John, 122, 123, 125; note 44
Sullivan, Gen. John, 127

T

Tallmadge, Maj. Benjamin, 134
Thomas, Gen. John, 115
Thompson, Benjamin, 71–80; notes 26, 27
Thompson, Mrs. Benjamin, 72, 73, 74
Thompson, Sarah, 74, 79
Townshend, Hon. Charles, 28

V

Van Wart, Isaac, 132, 140
Vardill, Rev. John, 91
Vergennes, Comte de, 153

W

Wallace, Capt., 46
Walpole, Horace, 162, 163
Ward, Henry, 47
Warren, Dr. Joseph, 42, 43, 44; note 15
Warren, Capt. Peter, 124
Washington, Gen. George, 4, 13, 42, 44, 47, 63, 75, 89, 99, 101, 103, 105, 114, 115, 127, 158, 162, 168; and Benedict Arnold, 136, 137, 142, 144; and Captain Huddy, 145, 148, 149, 150, 152, 153; note 56

Washington, Martha, 103
Wedderburn, Lord, 26
Weisenberg, Catherine, 124
Wentworth, Gov. John, 73
Wesley, Rev. John, 86
Wharton, Thomas, 57
White, Philip, 146
Whitney, Eli, 65
Wilkes, John, 28
Wilkinson, Gen. James, 65
Williams, David, 132, 140
Witherspoon, Rev. John, 129
Wolfe, Gen. James, 27
Woodhull, Rev. John, 148